Developing Quality Technical Information

A Handbook for Writers and Editors

GRETCHEN HARGIS ■ ANN KILTY HERNANDEZ ■ POLLY HUGHES
JIM RAMAKER ■ SHANNON ROUILLER ■ ELIZABETH WILDE

PRENTICE HALL PTR, UPPER SADDLE RIVER, NEW JERSEY 07458

Library of Congress Cataloging-in-Publication Data

Developing quality technical information : a handbook for writers and
    editors / Gretchen Hargis ... [et al.].
        p.   cm.
    Includes index.
    ISBN 0-13-790320-0 (paper)
    1. Technical writing. 2. Technical editing.   I. Hargis,
Gretchen.
T11.D417   1998   97-43384
808'.0666--dc21   CIP

Published by Prentice Hall PTR

Prentice-Hall, Inc.
A Simon & Schuster Company
Upper Saddle River, NJ 07458

Editorial/Production Supervision: James D. Gwyn
Acquisitions Editor: Michael E. Meehan
Manufacturing Manager: Alexis R. Heydt
Marketing Manager: Stephen Solomon
Cover Design Director: Jayne Conte
Cover Designers: Teresa Stoll, Tonya Rado, Bruce Kenselaar

Prentice Hall books are widely used by corporations and government agencies for training, marketing, and resale.
The publisher offers discounts on this book when ordered in bulk quantities. For more information, contact: Corporate Sales
Department, Phone: 800-382-3419; FAX: 201-236-7141; E-mail: corpsales@prenhall.com; or write: Prentice Hall PTR,
Corp. Sales Dept., One Lake Street, Upper Saddle River, NJ 07458.

Printed in the United States of America

10 9 8 7 6 5 4 3 2 1

ISBN 0-13-790320-0

Prentice-Hall International (UK) Limited, *London*
Prentice-Hall of Australia Pty. Limited, *Sydney*
Prentice-Hall Canada Inc., *Toronto*
Prentice-Hall Hispanoamericana, S.A., *Mexico*
Prentice-Hall of India Private Limited, *New Delhi*
Prentice-Hall of Japan, Inc., *Tokyo*
Simon & Schuster Asia Pte. Ltd., *Singapore*
Editora Prentice-Hall do Brasil, Ltda., *Rio de Janeiro*

Contents

Welcome!

Many books on technical writing tell you how to develop different parts of technical information, such as headings, lists, tables, and indexes. Instead, we organized this book to tell you how to apply quality characteristics that, in our experience, make technical information easy to use, easy to understand, and easy to find. We hope you will find our approach useful and comprehensive—and we hope you will find the information in this book easy to use, easy to understand, and easy to find!

Is this book for you?

If you are a writer or reviewer of technical information—yes! If you write or review software information, this book may be of even more interest to you because the examples in it come from the domain of software. However, the quality characteristics and guidelines are universal to all information.

Reviewers can be any of the many people who are involved in developing technical information:

❑ Writers
❑ Editors
❑ Graphic designers
❑ Human factors engineers
❑ Product developers and testers
❑ Customer service personnel
❑ Customers (perhaps as early users)
❑ Managers

In general, this book assumes that you know the basics of good grammar, punctuation, and spelling as they apply to writing. It does not assume that you are familiar with what makes technical information good or bad.

How to use this book

You can use the book in any of several ways:

- ❑ Read the book from start to finish.
- ❑ Read about the particular quality characteristic or guideline that interests you.
- ❑ Use the checklists at the end of each chapter and "Quality Checklist" on page 269 to evaluate a piece of technical information against the quality characteristics.
- ❑ Use "Who Checks Which Quality Characteristics?" on page 273 to see what areas you as a reviewer need to check, and read those sections.

Whatever your role in developing technical information, we hope that you'll use this information to build these quality characteristics into the information that you work on.

Changes in this edition

The first and second editions were published in 1984 and 1986 for use mainly by developers of information for IBM software products. This edition is published for more general use and takes into account these changes in technical information:

- ❑ Online information (such as help, tutorials, and documents) is often more important than printed information in the documentation of software.
- ❑ Online information has become more integrated with the product user interface, through forms such as cue cards and wizards.

As a result of comments from customers and editors, we have:

- ❑ Added two quality characteristics: concreteness and style

    Feedback from users showed that, to them, examples and scenarios are not only very important, but also generally lacking or poorly handled in computer information. The first edition treated examples as part of clarity, but clarity has many other aspects as well. In this edition we have added concreteness as the quality characteristic that focuses especially on examples and scenarios.

In the first edition, style considerations were spread across accuracy, clarity, and visual communication. We decided that style needs its own focus.

❏ Renamed two quality characteristics

The earlier name "entry points" has become "retrievability," and "visual communication" has become "visual effectiveness."

In addition, we have reorganized the book into parts and added several sections:

❏ Introduction to help define terms and set the context for the information
❏ Chapters 11 and 12, which treat more than one quality characteristic
❏ Annotated bibliography
❏ Glossary of terms used in this book
❏ Index

The technical editors at IBM's Santa Teresa Laboratory use these quality characteristics to assess the quality of the information they edit. In this edition, we have revised some guidelines and added more examples to ensure coverage of the kinds of common errors found every day.

Gretchen Hargis
Ann Kilty Hernandez
Polly Hughes
Jim Ramaker
Shannon Rouiller
Elizabeth Wilde

Acknowledgments

This book began in the 1980s at Santa Teresa Laboratory (STL) at IBM as *Producing Quality Technical Information*. Without the work of the writers and designers on that book, we probably would not have begun this project. For the quality they built into that book, we thank Dewey Beaudette, Fred Bethke, the late Bill Calhoun, Morris Dean, Polly Hughes, John Hurd, Terese Johnson, Kacy Keene, Lori Neumann, and Linda Stout.

In the early 1990s a quality work group at STL, under the direction of Ken Marks, pursued an idea that Ken had to extend the quality characteristics into a system for editing and evaluating technical information. In this group were Neale Barret, William Deason, Therese McQuillan, Jim Ramaker, and Elizabeth Wilde. We thank them for their efforts to launch this process.

The STL Editing Council, led by Jane Graves, continued the work of the quality work group by implementing systematic use of the quality characteristics when editing. We thank the people who pioneered that analysis and implementation, including Mary Aline, Martin Burch, Dan Dionne, Jim Gasiewski, Jane Graves, Chris Gray, Gretchen Hargis, George Heigho, Polly Hughes, Barbara Isa, Ken Jones, Tish Kuljian, Deirdre Longo, Ken Marks, Karen Merrell, Laura Nystrom, Joan Preston, Jim Ramaker, Stephanie Parkin, Mary Regan, Michelle Valdez, Elizabeth Wilde, and Fern Wollrich.

For her steadfast encouragement and support of this edition, we thank Lori Fisher, who raised the loudest cheers over every milestone reached. Lori also reviewed several drafts and used a draft of the book in a class that she teaches, helping to shape our work.

We lost a writer, Mary Regan, to medical school along the way, but we very much appreciate the work she did before leaving to pursue another dream.

We thank the editors' editor, Deirdre Longo, who juggled her product work to help us by editing a draft. Her comments led to many improvements.

Reviewers were an essential part of developing this book, giving us many useful comments on drafts. Our thanks to Shawn Benham, Lindsay Bennion, Barbara Bissinger, Dennis Bockus, Morris Dean, Irene Faivre, Roy Halliday, Jasna Krmpotic, Ken Marks, Lori Neumann, Thomas Sharp, Gayle Steinbugler, and Bob Turek.

Many thanks also to Patrick Kelley and Katherine McMurtrey, who joined the editors too late to get a major assignment but not too late to help out a lot. Wish you had come sooner!

For hours and hours of formatting work, we thank Michael Reddell, who helped immensely with the final preparation of the book. His keen eye and FrameMaker expertise helped make the elements look right on the pages.

Along with the writing, editing, reviewing, and production tasks were many business tasks. We thank Tina Woodward for the first clear vision and push to make this book available to a broader audience than IBM. We thank Bryan Patterson and Barbara Isa for their efforts to set up publishing agreements and clear the path of legal hassles. We thank William Deason for including us in meetings that he arranged with publishers.

We're grateful to Mike Meehan of Prentice Hall Professional Technical Reference (PTR) for seeing value and potential in our work and for shepherding the book through to broader availability.

Lastly we thank our families for their understanding when we worked evenings and weekends on this project.

If we missed or slighted someone in these acknowledgments, we didn't mean to.

Gretchen Hargis
Ann Kilty Hernandez
Polly Hughes
Jim Ramaker
Shannon Rouiller
Elizabeth Wilde

Chapter 1

Quality Technical Information

Technical information is the information that accompanies a product or describes something in a science (whether computer science, physical science, or social science), trade, or profession.

Technical information is not leisure reading for most people. Rather, they turn to technical information out of a need to know something, to solve a problem, probably as part of their job. Often they have little time to find the information they need.

Writers of technical information need to make the information easy to use, easy to understand, and easy to find.

This chapter contains the following information:

❑ Definition of quality technical information
❑ How to develop quality technical information

What is quality technical information?

Based on comments from users and experience in writing and editing technical information, we have found that quality technical information has these characteristics:

Accuracy	Freedom from mistakes or errors; adherence to fact or truth
Clarity	Freedom from ambiguity or obscurity
Completeness	The inclusion of all necessary parts—and only those parts
Concreteness	Freedom from abstraction; the inclusion of appropriate examples, scenarios, similes, and analogies
Organization	A coherent arrangement of parts that makes sense to the user
Retrievability	Presentation of information in a way that enables users to find specific items quickly and easily
Style	Correctness and appropriateness of writing conventions and choices in words and phrases
Task orientation	A focus on helping users complete the tasks associated with a product in relation to their jobs
Visual effectiveness	Attractiveness and enhanced meaning of information through use of layout, illustrations, color, type, icons, and other graphic devices

No one characteristic is sufficient to describe quality technical information, but each is necessary.

We can group these characteristics by their ability to make information:

- ❑ Easy to use—task orientation, accuracy, completeness
- ❑ Easy to understand—clarity, concreteness, and style
- ❑ Easy to find—organization, retrievability, and visual effectiveness

Each group focuses on the primary area where a quality characteristic helps, but it is not necessarily the only group where a characteristic could fit. For example, although visual effectiveness helps primarily with making technical information easy to find, it also helps make the information easy to understand and easy to use.

This book discusses how to achieve quality by applying each of the nine quality characteristics as you develop technical information.

Quality characteristics compared with elements and guidelines

Quality is difficult to identify, codify, or imitate. You cannot simply use headings, lists, and tables in the same way as they are in a document that you admire and achieve the same degree of quality. Yet, when you apply wise *guidelines* to the use of such *elements*, you can improve quality. In this book we use these terms with these meanings:

❑ *Elements* are the units that physically make up technical information. An element can be as small as a word and as large as a tutorial.

Paragraphs evolved as the primary element for conveying meaning in writing. Works of fiction tend to use paragraphs almost exclusively, plus maybe chapter titles and a table of contents, as clues to their structure. Technical information, however, requires more kinds of elements and liberal use of them. The paragraph becomes much less important as an element for conveying information. It becomes shorter and is broken up with lists, tables, and other means of differentiating information.

❑ *Guidelines* are brief directives about what to do or not do to achieve the characteristics of quality. These guidelines apply to the elements.

The quality characteristics of technical information are different from elements in these ways:

❑ Each quality characteristic expresses an innate goodness. The characteristics are not neutral, as are the elements.

Lists, for example, do not in themselves constitute quality technical information. Writers can use lists to achieve certain quality characteristics, such as clarity and retrievability. However, writers can also misuse lists—hence the need for guidelines about what to do and not do with lists.

❑ The information does not consist of the quality characteristics.

Writers cannot, for example, turn clarity on and off with a markup tag. Elements, however, do have recognizable limits and often have corresponding markup tags.

The elements span the quality characteristics (and vice versa), as shown in Table 7, "Quality Characteristics and Elements," on page 279.

You can see the guidelines for each quality characteristic in the table of contents.

Other possible quality characteristics of technical information

The characteristics that we have chosen are not the only possible quality characteristics of technical information. You might think of some other terms to define quality technical information, such as:

Conciseness   Brevity, succinctness; saying a lot in a few words

Consistency   Using the same elements or content where appropriate; agreement or logical coherence among parts

Preciseness   Clear expression; correctness to a fine degree

Readability   Ease of reading words and sentences

Relevance   Appropriateness to a subject

Simplicity   Freedom from complexity

However, clarity includes these characteristics. Clarity is broad enough to cover many characteristics and yet narrow enough to be different from the other characteristics we have chosen.

Some other possible characteristics are:

Adequacy   Just enough information; the right amount and kind of information to meet a need

Correctness   Freedom from mistakes or errors; this term is often used in technical writing in regard to matters of style

Honesty   Truthfulness, freedom from fraud or deceit

Usefulness   Capability of being used to advantage, of being of service

Again, the characteristics we have chosen can cover these:

❑ Accuracy includes correctness and honesty.

❏ Completeness includes adequacy.
❏ Style includes correctness.
❏ Task orientation includes usefulness.

Another very important characteristic of quality technical information is usability, or ease of use. We have used this characteristic as an umbrella for several other characteristics: task orientation, accuracy, and completeness.

How do I use the quality characteristics to develop quality technical information?

Developing quality technical information requires many skills, such as researching, interviewing, designing, writing, editing, reviewing, and usability testing. To cover these skills, probably more than one person is needed, though a writer can have many of these skills.

This book concentrates on the writing and reviewing skills.

Writing quality technical information is a complex task. You probably cannot achieve quality in one quick rush of words. In fact, a very important part of the writing process isn't writing at all, but preparing to write.

Preparing to write: understanding users, tasks, and the product

A writer needs to understand not only the product, writing tools, and the writing craft, but also certain facets of the typical user:

❏ Education and training
❏ Knowledge of the subject or related subjects
❏ Work environment

You need to build on the user's knowledge and speak the user's language. You can perform a *task analysis* to better understand your users and their tasks. You can monitor users as they work, interview them about their tasks, or survey a set of users. In a task analysis, you can focus on high-level tasks as well as on more detailed tasks.

The results of a task analysis can help you understand:

❏ Which tasks are most important to users

❑ Which tasks they spend the most time on
❑ Which tasks are most tedious or most trivial
❑ What type of organization is appropriate
❑ How much detail to include
❑ What kinds of examples to use

The more you understand about the users and their tasks, the easier it is for you to write relevant, task-oriented information.

If what you are writing about is new to you, pay close attention to your own questions and areas of confusion as you learn about the subject. The information you write might need to serve both the novice and the experienced user.

You need to understand how the product fits into what the user does and what new tasks the product requires of users. Above all, the users of your information are probably less interested in using the information or the product it represents than in doing their own work.

Many of the guidelines in this book speak of users as the reference point for decisions about what to write and how to write it.

Writing and rewriting

As with other kinds of writing, quality technical writing is a process of refinement. When you are first writing about a subject, just getting your thoughts on the screen or paper may be enough of a challenge. Striving at that point for quality characteristics such as retrievability and style might be more inhibiting than helpful.

You need not concentrate on achieving all of the quality characteristics at once. Some are more appropriate than others, depending on your approach and how far you are in developing the information. If you are starting by using a top-down approach (going from an outline to filling it in), you probably need to keep in mind the guidelines for task orientation and organization. If you are starting by using a bottom-up approach (writing pieces of information and then seeing how they fit together), the guidelines for clarity and visual effectiveness might be appropriate.

Eventually, as you develop the information, the guidelines for all the quality characteristics should come into play. Many of them need frequent consideration. Consider the clarity guideline "Use technical terms only if they are necessary and appropriate." Early in your writing, you might decide to use certain technical terms and then reconsider their use as you get feedback from users.

You need to revise sentences, paragraphs, procedures, and larger blocks of information, always bringing them closer to the goal of being accurate, clear, complete, concrete, well organized, easily retrievable, stylistically correct and appropriate, task oriented, and visually effective.

Part 1

Easy to Use

Ease of use is very broad. Some people equate it with usability, which they consider as broad as quality itself. Here we limit ease of use to the primary characteristics that determine whether users can actually apply the information. We distinguish this ability from being able to find and understand the information.

Chapter 2

Task Orientation

When you give users guidance information in a task-oriented way, you help them do their job. Essentially, task-oriented writing is writing in terms of how the user does the task.

You rarely help your users when you tell them how a product works or how it is structured internally. Your users have a job to do, so they need practical information—how-to information.

Try to perform task analysis for the tasks you're writing about. Task analysis can help you understand the tasks from your users' perspectives. You can use task analysis to improve traditional guidance information (printed documents or online help windows) and to identify tasks that warrant more interactive methods of guidance (such as interactive tutorials, cue cards, wizards, or instructional videos).

When you write guidance information, you are usually in a position to notice usability problems in time to suggest product improvements. For example, you might identify especially cumbersome steps that can be streamlined or avoided or steps where users are repeating actions that they've already performed (such as typing a long serial number in more than one window). If you have difficulty documenting a task, consider whether there might be a problem with the way the product works. Keep the needs and interests of your users in mind as you write; there is no such thing as a product that is too usable.

To make information task oriented, follow these guidelines:

- ❏ **Write for the intended audience.**
- ❏ **Present information from the user's point of view.**
- ❏ **Focus on real tasks, not product functions.**
- ❏ **Indicate a practical reason for information.**
- ❏ **Use titles and headings that reveal the tasks.**

Write for the intended audience

Before you start writing, be sure that you have a clear understanding of your audience. For example, if you are writing for managers, you probably want to include only high-level tasks, such as evaluating and planning, or a high-level view of other tasks; and if you are writing for system administrators, you want to avoid application programming tasks.

Before you add information to a document, be sure your audience is interested in the information. For example, your product might have a powerful new help system, but information about the help system is of little interest to the person who is reading about installation.

The following passage shows a simple task explained in detail. However, the audience consists of users who want to use an advanced feature and therefore do not need help performing simple tasks. This information will frustrate all but the most patient advanced user.

Original

> To use the advanced setup:
>
> 1. Go to the file tree.
> 2. Click the INFODIR folder.
> 3. Drag the ADVANCE.SET file from the INFODIR folder to the MYDIR folder.
> 4. Drop the ADVANCE.SET file into the MYDIR folder.
> 5. Close the file tree.

Revision

> To use the advanced setup, copy the ADVANCE.SET file from the INFODIR directory to your directory.

In the revision, the task is handled much more simply. The revision quickly provides the users with the information they need, because the writer understands the skill level of the audience.

Present information from the user's point of view

Writing from the user's point of view brings the user into the "story," so it is easy for the user to imagine doing what you are describing. Such writing is predominantly directed at "you" (second person). It uses the active voice, with verbs that denote actions the *user* does as opposed to actions the product does. It also gives a reason for those actions.

Original

> The system should not be shut down during processing. If this happens, the system should be restarted with the START /RECOVER command.

Revision

> If you shut down the system during processing, you might lose data. Use the START /RECOVER command to restart the system and recover any data from the log.

The original passage is written from a remote, impersonal point of view. It is passive and indefinite about who does the action and why. In the revision, the information is presented to make the user an active participant. Like fiction writing, it indicates motivation: the phrase, "you might lose data," expresses the reason for the action in terms users can relate to personally— they don't *want* to lose data.

The following passage has nothing to do with the users:

Original

> Subsequent installation of the HIGS feature allows InfoProduct to run unattended.

Revision

> If you want to run InfoProduct unattended, you need to install the HIGS feature. You can install the HIGS feature after you install InfoProduct.

The original passage leaves the users out of the story altogether. The information is there, but the users don't know how it pertains to them. The revision adds the users to the story and explains what they need to *do* to use the feature.

When users access online help for a product window, they probably want to know how to interact with the window to perform their task. When you provide task help, you have the advantage of knowing where the users are in the interface and, therefore, what part of the task they need help with.

For the following help windows, suppose a user accesses online help from the Primary Key page (which is the third and final page) of the Create Table notebook.

Original

> To create a table:
>
> 1. Select the **Table** object from the tree.
>
> 2. Click mouse button 2 on the **Table** object and select **Create** from the pop-up menu. The Create Table notebook opens.
>
> 3. On the Table page of the notebook, specify a name for the table.
>
> 4. On the Columns page of the notebook, specify the names and types of columns for the table.
>
> 5. On the Primary Key page of the notebook, specify a column to be the primary key.
>
>   a. Select the column you want to define as the primary key column for your new table from the **Columns** list box.
>
>   b. Click the **>** push button to move the selected column to the **Primary key** list box.
>
> 6. Click **OK**. InfoBase creates the table.

Revision

> Use this page of the notebook to define a primary key. You need to define a primary key when you create a table.
>
> Before you define a primary key, you must specify a name for the table and the names and types of its columns.
>
> To define a primary key:
>
> 1. Select the column you want to define as the primary key column for your new table from the **Columns** list box.
>
> 2. Click the **>** push button to move the selected column to the **Primary key** list box.
>
> When you've defined the primary key, click **OK** to close the notebook. InfoBase creates the table based on the information you specified in the notebook.

The revised help window presents the task from the user's probable position. The user has already completed most of the steps of the "Creating a table" task and needs only information on the "Specifying the primary key" subtask.

Focus on real tasks, not product functions

A *real task* is a task users want to perform, whether or not they are using your product to do it. It is all too easy in technical writing to lose sight of the real tasks and get caught up in the tasks dictated by the product. When you live and breathe a product for months, you forget that the user's tasks and the product's tasks are not necessarily the same. Tasks that are imposed by the product are called *artificial tasks*. Examples of real and artificial tasks are:

❑ Users want to edit a table; but the writer introduces this task as "using the table editor" instead of "editing a table."

❑ Users want to count the records in a file; but the writer introduces the task as "using the CNTREC utility" instead of "counting records with the CNTREC utility."

Sometimes a product's design forces you to write about artificial tasks. For example, users want to create a graphic, but must first set up containers to hold sets of graphics. In such cases, you can focus on the task rather than the design by writing about "organizing your graphics with containers" rather than "creating containers."

In the following task introduction, the writer makes the common mistake of describing the task in product-specific terms.

Original

> To use the InfoInstaller utility:
>
> 1. Type `infoinst` at the command line. The InfoInstaller window opens.
> 2. Specify the installation parameters in the window.
> 3. Click **OK**. InfoProduct is installed.

Revision

> To install InfoProduct:
>
> 1. Type `infoinst` at the command line. The InfoInstaller window opens.
>
>   InfoInstaller is a tool that helps automate the installation process.
>
> 2. Specify the installation parameters in the window.
>
> 3. Click **OK**. The InfoProduct is installed.

The original introduction assumes the users understand the task in terms of the tool they use to perform the task. Although some users might know what InfoInstaller is, *all* users know what installation is. The revised introduction and steps separate the task from the tool so that the users can relate the real task of installing to the tool they use to install.

The following introduction shows a chapter that is systematically explaining how to use the product rather than how to perform real tasks with the product.

Original

> This chapter explains how to use the following menu choices under **File**:
>
> **Open**   Opens an existing file. See page 5.
> **New**   Creates a file. See page 5.
> **Save as**   Saves to a new file with a different name. See page 6.

Revision

> This chapter explains how to:
>
> ❑ Create a document
> ❑ Open an existing document
> ❑ Rename a document

The original text assumes that the user is examining the interface and wondering what each menu item does. This type of information is appropriate for *contextual help* (help that is relevant to where a user is in a product, such as help for the selected menu choice), but not for a user's guide. Users want information about how to perform real tasks, not a list of the buttons and controls in the product. The revision shows information presented in terms of real tasks.

By presenting the information from the perspective of tasks that users recognize and want to perform, you make your information more relevant to your users.

The following help window presents the task in terms of the window that is used to perform the task:

Original

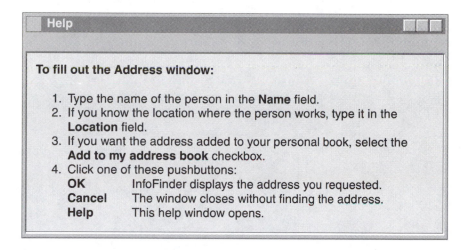

To fill out the Address window:

1. Type the name of the person in the **Name** field.
2. If you know the location where the person works, type it in the **Location** field.
3. If you want the address added to your personal book, select the **Add to my address book** checkbox.
4. Click one of these pushbuttons:
   OK   InfoFinder displays the address you requested.
   Cancel   The window closes without finding the address.
   Help   This help window opens.

Revision

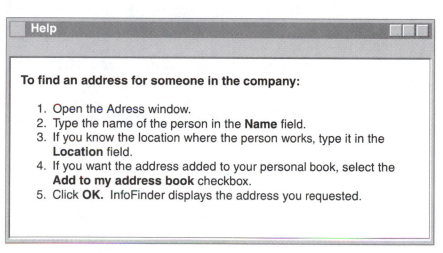

To find an address for someone in the company:

1. Open the Adress window.
2. Type the name of the person in the **Name** field.
3. If you know the location where the person works, type it in the **Location** field.
4. If you want the address added to your personal book, select the **Add to my address book** checkbox.
5. Click **OK.** InfoFinder displays the address you requested.

The original help window tells the user how to use the *window*; it explains how to fill out the window, but it never explains what real task the user is performing. The original help window also contains extraneous information about the window that isn't pertinent to the real task.

The revised help window presents the information in terms of the task the user wants to perform and lists the steps that are involved in the task.

Keep your task steps focused on the real task. Avoid littering your steps with little feature "advertisements" unless the features are especially helpful to the user as part of the task. The following help window contains unnecessary features mixed in as part of the task:

Original

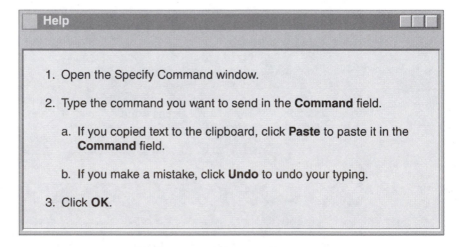

Help

1. Open the Specify Command window.

2. Type the command you want to send in the **Command** field.

   a. If you copied text to the clipboard, click **Paste** to paste it in the **Command** field.

   b. If you make a mistake, click **Undo** to undo your typing.

3. Click **OK**.

Revision

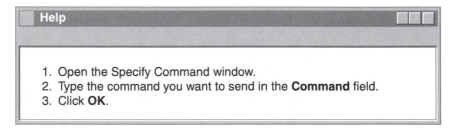

Help

1. Open the Specify Command window.
2. Type the command you want to send in the **Command** field.
3. Click **OK**.

Steps 2a and 2b in the original help window are *not* part of the task. They are only features that users can use; if you document every feature like this, your tasks will become unwieldy and lose their focus.

Indicate a practical reason for information

Giving users the information they need is only part of task-oriented writing. Users need a practical reason for the information. They need to understand *why* you are giving it to them—how it is relevant to their task. The goal that the information serves must be apparent. A task is not just an activity, but an activity that is directed to a particular end.

Relate conceptual information to tasks where appropriate

Users should never wonder, "But why are you telling me this?" For example, to state that the records in a file have a certain size might leave users wondering, "So what?"

But if you tell them that they will have to build a library to hold the file (and if you tell them how record size affects the way they do this), they can understand why you are telling them about record size.

Raw facts can puzzle users if you don't indicate what significance the facts have, as shown in the following passage.

Original

> If the NORES option was used, the routines are link-edited as part of the load module. If the RES option was used, the routines are loaded separately.

Revision

> Use the NORES option when you have sufficient space for routines to be link-edited as part of your load module. Use the RES option to save space by loading the routines only when you need them.

The original passage explains what the options do, but does not relate that information to the users' task of deciding which option to use. In the revision, the facts are restated so the users understand when to use which option.

At first glance, the following sentence appears to be totally conceptual and have no practical application.

Original

> The MSG mapping table of the DATALM directory can contain warning messages that are issued by InfoProduct when you create a request.

Revision

> After you create a request, check the MSG mapping table to see if InfoProduct issued any warning messages. The MSG mapping table is in the DATALM directory.

Users might glance at the original sentence and move on because it doesn't seem relevant. The revised sentence relates the information to the task of creating a request, so users understand why the information is significant.

Provide only the appropriate amount of conceptual information

Avoid presenting too much conceptual information before presenting a task. You might be able to merge the conceptual information in with the task steps. You might also consider using headings to separate the conceptual information from the task steps.

Users want to learn to do things without having to learn all the concepts behind a product. Provide steps as early as possible, and provide concepts only when necessary.

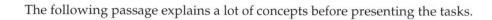

The following passage explains a lot of concepts before presenting the tasks.

Original

> Projects are collections of files related to one main test case. When you create a main test case, you must also create a project. You can, however, create a project before you create a main test case. Each project can contain multiple test cases, but only one main test case. You create projects in suites. Each suite can contain multiple projects. It's a good idea to create one suite for each function you are testing. The projects in that suite can contain the main test cases you create to test that function.
>
> To create a suite:
>
> 1.
> 2.
>
> To create a project:
>
> 1.
> 2.
>
> To create a test case:
>
> 1.
> 2.

Revision

> Creating Test Cases
>
> You can create two types of test cases: a main test case (one that calls other test cases) or a regular test case. It's helpful to create the main test case first.
>
> Before you begin, you must:
>
> 1. Create a suite for the function you are testing.
>   a.
>   b.
> 2. Create a project within the suite to hold the main test case and all other related test cases and files.
>   a.
>   b.
>
> To create a main test case:
>
> 1. Select **Test Case -> New** from the Project window.
> 2.

The original passage starts with a lot of conceptual information about projects and then tells the user how to create all the needed elements. The revised passage pulls some of the conceptual information into the task description (including the before-you-begin steps) to make more sense of the conceptual information as it relates to the task.

23

Use titles and headings that reveal the tasks

The first place to tell users why they are being given information is in the title or heading. From a heading, users expect to get an accurate idea about the material that immediately follows.

Headings are elements that users use to locate information. Therefore, this guideline is related to retrievability as well as task orientation.

A static heading like "Authorizations" may be fine for reference information, but for guidance information, the heading should reveal the task users are being told how to do. A more helpful heading might be "Authorizing Users" or "Getting the Required Authorizations for a User ID."

Task-oriented titles and headings are essential for guidance information. Not only must there be a sufficient number of headings, but each heading should reveal that the section that follows contains information about a task, and what the task is.

Be careful not to mislead users by using *pseudo-task* headings. Pseudo-task headings start with vague verbs, such as "understanding" and "learning" (and sometimes "using"), and are often used to:

❏ Make a section sound task-oriented when it is actually full of reference information. For example, a section called "Understanding the File System" probably does not contain steps on how to understand the file system, but instead contains a lot of conceptual information about the file system. A more appropriate heading might be simply "The File System."

❏ Substitute a real task with an artificial (product-imposed) task. For example, a heading like "Using the SpellMaster Tool" is hiding the real task, and should probably be called "Checking the Spelling in a Document" instead. "Focus on real tasks, not product functions" on page 17 provides more discussion and examples of real and artificial tasks.

Good headings produce a good table of contents, from which users can predict what they will find in each section: guidance or reference information.

The following headings are misleading and unhelpful.

Original

> **Register Usage**
> **Administering Authorization**
> **The Dial-up Function**
> **Session Initialization**
> **Using the Define Font Window**
> **Understanding Hardware Requirements**

Revision

> **Linking with Registers**
> **Authorizing Access to Data**
> **Dialing Up the Computer**
> **Initializing a Session**
> **Defining a Font**
> **Hardware Requirements**

Some of the original headings hide the fact that guidance information follows; others define the tasks in terms of the product; and the last heading misrepresents a reference section as a guidance section. The revised headings clearly reveal the kind of information that follows; they use verbs that express user actions, and they indicate the goal of the action. Only indirectly (if at all) do they indicate the tool used.

The revised headings use gerunds for task-oriented headings. Gerunds are not the only alternative for task-oriented headings. You might also choose to use headings like "How to Define a Font" or "Steps for Defining a Font."

In sum

Use the guidelines in this chapter to ensure that technical information is task oriented. Refer to the examples in the chapter for practical applications of these guidelines.

When you review technical information for task orientation, you can use this checklist in two ways:

❏ As a reminder of what to look for, to ensure a thorough review
❏ As an evaluation tool, to determine the quality of the information

You can apply the quality rating in the third column of the checklist to the guideline as a whole. Judging by the number and severity of items you found, decide how the information rates on each guideline for this quality characteristic. You can then add your findings to "Quality Checklist" on page 269, which covers all the quality characteristics.

Although the guidelines are intended to cover all areas for this quality characteristic, you might find additional items to add to the list for a guideline.

Guidelines for task orientation	Items to look for	Quality rating
Write for the intended audience.	• Tasks are appropriate for the intended audience. • Audience is clearly defined. • Audience is clearly addressed. • Level of assumed preparation is consistent.	1 2 3 4 5
Present information from the user's point of view.	• Information is presented from the user's point of view. • Online help is presented from the user's position.	1 2 3 4 5
Focus on real tasks, instead of product functions.	• Information focuses on real tasks, not artificial tasks. • Tasks contain only information that pertains to the main task. • Focus is on tasks, not features and interface.	1 2 3 4 5
Indicate a practical reason for information.	• Conceptual information supports the task. • The minimum amount of conceptual information is presented before a task.	1 2 3 4 5
Use titles and headings that reveal the tasks.	• The title of guidance information identifies the task. • Headings reveal tasks. • There are no pseudo-task headings.	1 2 3 4 5

Note: The scale for the quality rating goes from very satisfied (1) to very dissatisfied (5).

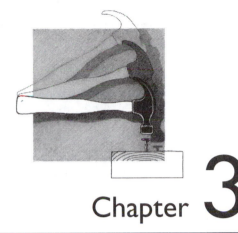

Accuracy

As writers of technical information, you have an important responsibility: to provide information that is accurate—free of errors. Users depend on you for that accuracy; they stake their time and money on it.

For technical information to be accurate, every piece of information must be accurate, including conceptual information, factual statements, procedures, graphical elements, and other details in the writing.

Inaccuracies might or might not be obvious. Those that aren't obvious are more significant, because the user might take action based on inaccurate information.

For example, imagine someone leaving a message on your answering machine with directions to "turn right at the dead end." Before you get in your car, you know this is incorrect because you can't turn right at a dead end. Therefore you take steps to resolve the inaccuracy, like looking at a map or asking for clarification.

If the person's message says "turn right at Front Street and go straight until you cross the railroad tracks," you could drive for quite some time before realizing that no railroad tracks are in this direction, and that you were actually supposed to turn left instead of right. You'll probably be more upset by the second set of directions than the first.

Regardless of how long it takes users to detect an inaccuracy, their confidence in the information is eroded; they might even choose not to use the information or the product at all.

To make information accurate, follow these guidelines:

- ❏ **Write only information that you understand, and verify it.**
- ❏ **Run tools that automate accuracy checking.**
- ❏ **Keep up with changes in the product.**
- ❏ **Maintain consistency of all information on a given topic.**
- ❏ **Check the accuracy of references to related information.**

Write only information that you understand, and verify it

You must understand a topic well enough that you can tell users what they need to know. You don't need to understand the topic as well as the programmers of the product. In fact, if you understand the internal workings of the product too well, you run the risk of including more information than the users need. ("Completeness" on page 49 provides guidelines for knowing how much information is needed.)

If you understand what you're writing about, you'll be better able to clearly explain concepts and define terms, as in the following list of terms for an object-oriented product.

Original

| class | A group or set of entities that share similar attributes. |
| method | A way to do something. |

Revision

| class | A template that you use to define the implementation of similar entities. Each class has a name and probably also attributes and methods. |
| method | An interface to a procedure that client application programs use to perform operations on data values of a class. |

The writer of the original list of terms and definitions doesn't understand the object-oriented meanings of the terms, so the definitions are inaccurate in the object-oriented context. In the revised list, the writer accurately explains the terms.

The best way to understand a product you are writing about is to use it as a user would. The more that you, as a writer, can use the product, the more responsible you can be for the accuracy of the information. For example, after writing a procedure for creating a database view that is based on two tables, you can test that procedure; if you successfully create the view, you know the procedure is accurate. When time allows, schedule a usability walkthrough in which you and other writers use the information to perform some or all of the important user tasks.

Even writers who use the product extensively while they are writing must seek feedback from:

❑ Technical reviewers, on accuracy of technical information
❑ The writing team, on accuracy of nontechnical information

You can solicit this feedback informally, while you are writing small parts of your information, as well as formally, when you hold reviews or inspections.

Run tools that automate accuracy checking

Many tools are available to help writers identify certain types of errors such as typographical errors, grammatical errors, and invalid cross-references.

A typographical error can become a major accuracy problem, such as when the error is in a code example, user procedure, statement of valid values, or syntax definition, as in the following diagram.

Original

Revision

In the original syntax diagram, the keyword is misspelled as REPLAC. A user who specifies the incorrect keyword will probably receive an error message about an unknown keyword. The revised syntax diagram accurately spells the keyword as REPLACE.

Although tools for checking spelling can find misspelled words and repeated words, they will not help you find places where you have the wrong word. For example, you might have accidentally typed *their* instead of *there*, or *though* instead of *through*. A spell checker does not consider whether a word makes sense in context, but only whether it is spelled as in the dictionary that the tool uses. A tool that checks for passive constructions, vague referents, and other syntax problems might help with finding such accuracy problems.

Keep up with changes in the product

Technical information that is not current is inaccurate. Information can become outdated from one release to the next, or within a given development cycle.

Each time you publish a new edition of your information, make sure that trademarks, product names and release levels, and other boilerplate information are current. Try to avoid mentioning specific release levels of products unless you have a valid technical reason to do so, such as:

❑ Marketing information that highlights the features of a new release or version of a product

❑ Restrictions that apply to a specific release

The following help window gives a specific release level, which is unnecessary.

Original

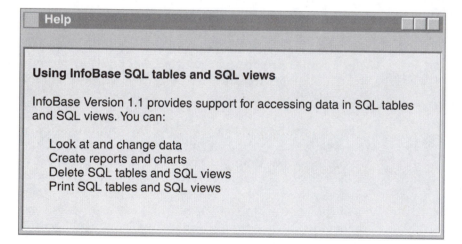

Revision

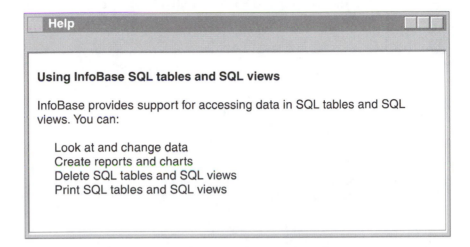

Using InfoBase SQL tables and SQL views

InfoBase provides support for accessing data in SQL tables and SQL views. You can:

Look at and change data
Create reports and charts
Delete SQL tables and SQL views
Print SQL tables and SQL views

Specifying the release number for a product, as in the original help window, might be accurate for this release, but it could look inaccurate if it's not changed in the next release. If a product will continue to provide capabilities, write about them in a general way, as in the revised help window.

Information can also become outdated during the development cycle for a product, even before it is available. For example, when a product has a specifications document, writers tend to incorporate information from it. However, this document can get out of sync with the actual product, even if the team documents design changes. Changes creep in, and people forget to mention them.

Ensure that your own information accurately describes the product by checking that the information matches what users will see and experience.

Original

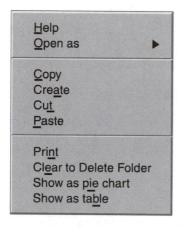

Revision

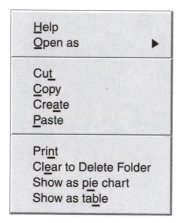

Suppose that the specification included the original menu, with the Cut, Copy, and Create choices in that sequence. A writer who assumes the specification is correct and includes this menu in information for users would be creating an accuracy problem. A writer who checks the actual menu can detect the error and correct the menu in the user information, as shown in the revised menu.

Maintain consistency in all information on a given topic

Many accuracy problems occur because the writer updates information in one place but not in other places where it appears. Faced with inconsistent information, the user doesn't know which information is correct.

When you determine that it's necessary to repeat, word for word, a specific piece of information (sometimes called a "chunk"), you can take advantage of the best way to ensure information consistency: reuse the information.

To reuse information, you can use either of these approaches:

❑ Embed the information
❑ Copy the information

Whether you embed or copy information, accuracy is best served if you do not change the reused information in content or format. However, changes are sometimes needed, such as to make a procedure fit a different operating system. Then embedding information is preferable because you can add conditional coding to the original to include or exclude certain information. Embedding is also preferable because it involves sharing common information. When updates are needed, you can make the changes in one place, rather than having to change the copies also.

Unless otherwise noted, reuse in this book means the sharing of common information, not the copying of information.

Reuse information when possible

By reusing common information, you ensure that the user is not confused about what is correct. You also need to change that information only one time.

The following table shows several ways that you can reuse information.

Opportunity for reuse	Method for reuse
Help text for various interface elements used on multiple windows	Single source for common help text, used by various windows via links
Text of messages, used by the product as it invokes messages and in printed information	Common source file for message text, called by product and embedded by book's formatter

Opportunity for reuse	Method for reuse
Information on the Web and in printed format	Common source file, formatted separately for Web and printed delivery vehicles
Online help and related printed information	Common source file for technical information chunks, called by product and embedded by book's formatter
Boilerplate text for the front matter of multiple books	Common source file for boilerplate text, embedded by the formatter of multiple books

Not only does using a common or single source file improve the accuracy of information, but it also eliminates the time needed to synchronize similar information.

Manually synchronize related information that doesn't match

Unfortunately, not all related information can be reused. Writers must manually synchronize related information that can't be reused.

A good rule of thumb is to minimize the number of places you write about a given piece of information. For example:

❑ In a procedure that requires the user to enter the same command more than once, consider giving the full syntax only once (TRACE SYSTEM INFOBASE NEW DEBUG LOG=YES), and then referring to it elsewhere as "the TRACE command shown in step 1." If you repeat the command in each place, you risk inconsistency that might make the user unsure of which format is correct.

❑ When you're writing for the Web and want to repeat information from another Web site you don't control, you can either:

— Paraphrase the content and link to it. The advantage to this approach is that when the information changes (as it is bound to do), you won't need to update it on your Web page, and you won't be responsible for an inconsistency that is perceived as an inaccuracy. The disadvantages are degraded performance for users who need the information and the risk that the linked-to Web page will disappear, causing a broken link.

— Copy the information to your Web page. The advantage to this approach is improved performance for users who need the information. The disadvantage is that you need to keep your copy of the information in sync with the original copy.

Whenever two related pieces of information are inconsistent, the user's confusion is like your confusion in using a recipe that starts with "Preheat the oven to 325°" and ends with "Bake at 375° for 40 minutes." You don't know which temperature is correct.

Sometimes you need to include technical information in more than one place, often in more than one format. Syntax diagrams and their supporting parameter lists are one example of a situation that requires some overlap of technical information, as in the following passage.

Original

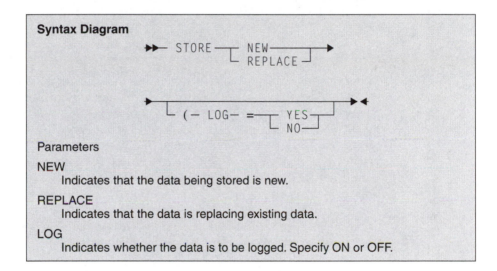

Syntax Diagram

Parameters

NEW
    Indicates that the data being stored is new.

REPLACE
    Indicates that the data is replacing existing data.

LOG
    Indicates whether the data is to be logged. Specify ON or OFF.

Revision

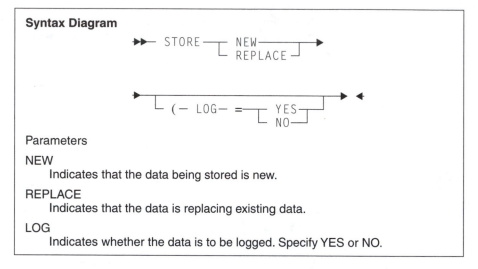

Syntax Diagram

Parameters

NEW
    Indicates that the data being stored is new.

REPLACE
    Indicates that the data is replacing existing data.

LOG
    Indicates whether the data is to be logged. Specify YES or NO.

In the original passage, the syntax diagram indicates that the LOG parameter should be set to YES or NO, but the parameter list indicates that the LOG parameter should be ON or OFF. Either seems plausible, so the user is left to figure it out by trial and error. This kind of error frequently occurs when the writer learns from a technical expert that the keyword has changed. The writer makes the change in one place but not in another. This kind of error would not be caught by most automated tools that check for spelling and grammatical errors.

The writer of the revised passage has synchronized the related information. The syntax diagram and parameter list are consistent.

A habit that can help you maintain the consistency of related information is to ask, each time you make any change to an existing file: "Should I be making any other changes as a result of this one?" Consciously asking yourself this question might help you think of other parts of your information that need to be changed.

Other inaccuracies occur when the names or headings of various elements are incorrect, such as when the content of a figure or table is inconsistent with its caption or surrounding text. Headings should accurately describe the content of the section. The column headings of a table should be consistent with and accurately reflect the actual content of the column's cells. Window titles should accurately reflect the content of the window.

Original

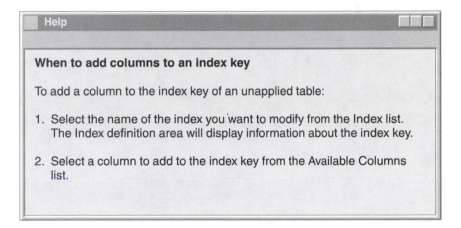

Help

When to add columns to an index key

To add a column to the index key of an unapplied table:

1. Select the name of the index you want to modify from the Index list. The Index definition area will display information about the index key.

2. Select a column to add to the index key from the Available Columns list.

Revision

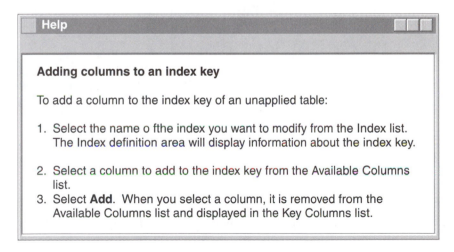

Help

Adding columns to an index key

To add a column to the index key of an unapplied table:

1. Select the name o fthe index you want to modify from the Index list. The Index definition area will display information about the index key.

2. Select a column to add to the index key from the Available Columns list.
3. Select **Add**. When you select a column, it is removed from the Available Columns list and displayed in the Key Columns list.

The heading of the original help window implies that the window explains the conditions under which a user would add columns to an index key. The revised help window has a heading that more accurately indicates the content of the window. Mislabeled information can also cause retrievability problems.

When you provide guidelines or rules for users, and you include an example to support those guidelines, make sure your example follows the guidelines, as in the following reference information on the DATE command.

Original

DATE command

Syntax

date *mm.dd.yyyy*

Parameter

mm.dd.yyyy

Sets the date. Values for the month and day must each be two characters. A value for the year must be four characters. The values must be separated by periods.

Example

`5.24.01`

Revision

DATE command

Syntax

date *mm.dd.yyyy*

Parameter

mm.dd.yyyy

Sets the date. Values for the month and day must each be two characters. A value for the year must be four characters. The values must be separated by periods.

Example

`05.24.2001`

In the original passage, the rules say that the values for month and day must each be two characters and the year value must be four characters. However, the example shows the month as one character and the year as two characters. The example in the revised passage shows the month and year correctly. This type of inaccuracy is especially problematic, because many users focus on examples and don't read the surrounding text.

Check the accuracy of references to related information

These are the kinds of references that you need to pay particular attention to:

❏ **References to Web locations.** Unless your information is updated quarterly (or more often), consider using company or organizational URLs instead of more specific subsidiary URLs, which are likely to change much more frequently.

❏ **References to printed material.** This includes the title and author or publisher.

❏ **Internal cross-references.** For online and Web information, the desired information must be at the end of a link. For printed information, internal cross-references must take the user to the desired information. Publishing software takes care of most cross-reference problems by dynamically rebuilding cross-references, but you still need to check that the referred-to section contains the information you want the user to find.

Whenever you update your information, verify all existing references. Sometimes, information you reference in another book might have moved.

Accuracy

A link on the following Web page is inaccurate.

Original

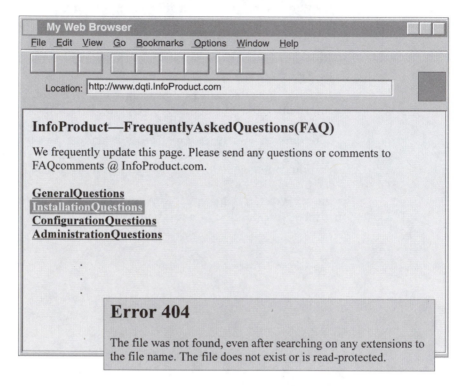

In the original Web page, the link to the Installation Questions Web page fails and results in an error message to the user. The link in the following revised Web page works as designed and takes the user to the desired information.

44

Developing Quality Technical Information

Revision

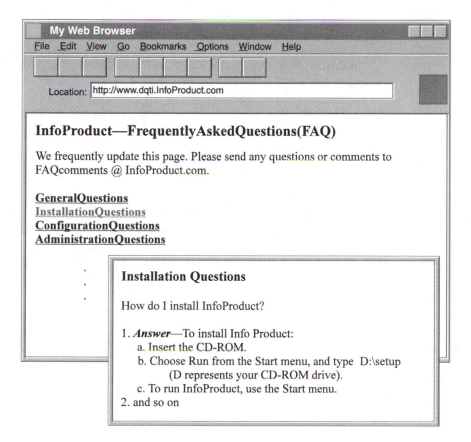

In sum

Use the guidelines in this chapter to ensure that technical information is accurate. Refer to the examples in the chapter for practical applications of these guidelines.

When you review technical information for accuracy, you can use this checklist in two ways:

❑ As a reminder of what to look for, to ensure a thorough review
❑ As an evaluation tool, to determine the quality of the information

You can apply the quality rating in the third column of the checklist to the guideline as a whole. Judging by the number and severity of items you found, decide how the information rates on each guideline for this quality characteristic. You can then add your findings to "Quality Checklist" on page 269, which covers all the quality characteristics.

Although the guidelines are intended to cover all areas for this quality characteristic, you might find additional items to add to the list for a guideline.

Guidelines for accuracy	Items to look for	Quality rating
Write only information that you understand, and verify it.	• Interface descriptions are consistent with the actual interface. • Procedures are correct; they work when a user follows them.	1 2 3 4 5
Run tools that automate accuracy checking.	• Examples, syntax descriptions, procedures, and other information chunks are free of spelling errors. • Text is free of grammatical errors.	1 2 3 4 5
Keep up with changes in the product.	• Trademark lists are current. • References to specific products are current.	1 2 3 4 5
Maintain consistency of all information on a given topic.	• Redundant information (which should match) is consistent. • No conflicts exist between separate but related pieces of information, such as: — Syntax diagrams agree with supporting parameter lists. — Headings accurately describe the content of the sections. — Figure and table captions accurately describe the contents. — Table column headings accurately describe the content of the column's cells. — Help window titles accurately reflect the content of the windows. — Guidelines or rules are accurately followed in related examples.	1 2 3 4 5
Check the accuracy of references to related information.	• Cross-references are correct. (Online or Web links work as designed, and printed cross-references point to the correct page.) • Cited information (Web, online, or printed) contains the relevant information. • Titles or order numbers are correctly cited.	1 2 3 4 5

Note: The scale for the quality rating goes from very satisfied (1) to very dissatisfied (5).

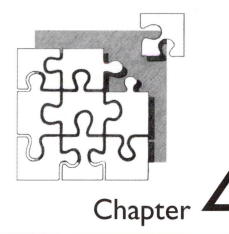

Chapter 4

Completeness

Completeness, from the user's point of view, means that all the information needed to perform a task is contained in the document or online text. A topic is covered completely when all the relevant topics are covered, each topic is covered in sufficient detail, and all the promised information is included.

Creating the right amount of information is a balancing act. You add or subtract information as you learn, through task analysis and by using the product, exactly what information users need. Performing usability tests can help you identify problems related to too much information, missing information, or both.

You need to understand the purpose of the information you are creating. For example, will users be performing a specific task? Learning concepts? Making a decision?

Writers have often created technical information that is *too* complete, including everything there is to know about a product. Today, the trend in technical writing is toward providing the user with far less information, an approach called minimalism. The minimalist approach not only yields a reduction in page count, but it also results in writing that doesn't get in the user's way. With a minimum of information, the user can independently explore a product after learning some basic concepts and tasks.

To make information complete, follow these guidelines:

- ❑ **Cover all topics that support users' tasks, and only those topics.**
- ❑ **Cover each topic in just as much detail as users need.**
- ❑ **Use patterns of information to ensure proper coverage.**
- ❑ **Repeat information only when users will benefit from it.**

Cover all topics that support users' tasks, and only those topics

Users of technical information almost always need guidance information on how to perform their tasks. This guideline is related to the quality characteristic of task orientation, because you cannot decide what topics must be covered without evaluating the tasks that users are to perform.

The minimal topics for guidance information are descriptions of the major user tasks, their subtasks, and the reasons or conditions for performing them. Early in your writing project, do a task analysis to determine what tasks and subtasks your users will need to perform. Later in the project, you can use the task analysis to evaluate whether your information covers the necessary topics. Have you covered all major user tasks? Have you described all the subtasks that users need to perform to complete the major tasks? Have you explained the reasons or conditions associated with optional tasks? If you can answer these questions, your information is more likely to cover all the topics the user needs.

In the following table of contents, an important word-processing subtask of working with a file is omitted, probably because the writer failed to identify the users' subtasks.

Original

> **Working with an InfoWrite file**
> Creating a new file to edit
> Working with text
>   Selecting text
>   Inserting text
>   Overwriting text
>   Deleting text
>   Highlighting text
>   Locating text
>   Moving text
>   Copying text
> Opening an existing file
> **Printing a file**

Revision

Working with an InfoWrite file
Creating a new file to edit
Working with text
  Selecting text
  Inserting text
  Overwriting text
  Deleting text
  Highlighting text
  Locating text
  Moving text
  Copying text
Saving a file
Opening an existing file
Printing a file

Although most users of word-processing programs want to save their work, the original table of contents omits the step of saving a file from the section on working with a file. The revised table of contents includes this important subtask.

Sometimes you need to explain concepts as you introduce a topic, explain a process, or highlight benefits. However, you need to make sure that the user really needs the conceptual information. Ask yourself what the user will do with the information. For example, will the information help the user make a decision or perform a task? While installing, users probably need information about the installation options so they can decide which ones they need and what values to choose. While evaluating details about product license, users need boilerplate information about the licensing agreement. Information that you can't relate to a user need is probably extraneous.

In the following passage, the writer has included a lengthy list of message identifiers, even though the list doesn't help users with any task.

Original

Reporting an error message problem

Each InfoTool message has an identifier. Message identifiers that begin with ABU indicate programming errors that you can probably correct without help from a service representative. For information about ABU messages and how to correct the errors, see *InfoTool Programming Reference*.

When you receive an error message, follow these steps:

1. Check the third letter of the message identifier. If the letter is U (as in ABU1114E), see Step 2. If the letter is S (as in ABS1225E), see Step 3.

2. If the third letter is U, you can probably fix the problem yourself. For help with a particular message, see *InfoTool Programming Reference*, which lists all InfoTool messages.

3. If the third letter is S, call 1-800-555-1111 and tell the representative the message identifier. The representative will work with you to resolve the problem quickly. All 150 ABS messages are listed below:

ABS1112E	ABS1118E	ABS1132E	ABS1218E	ABS2111E
ABS1113E	ABS1119E	ABS1133E	ABS1219E	ABS2112E
ABS1114E	ABS1120E	ABS1134E	ABS1220E	ABS2113E
ABS1115E	ABS1121E	ABS1135E	ABS1221E	ABS2114E
ABS1116E	ABS1122E	ABS1136E	ABS1222E	ABS2115E

and so on

The original passage lists all 150 ABS messages that the InfoTool product issues, even though users can't independently correct the problems these messages identify. Not only is this a potential accuracy problem (as new messages are added to the product), but it also makes the information longer than it needs to be and does not help users.

The following revised passage excludes the list of messages, which in this case is extraneous, and efficiently tells users what to do if they receive an ABS message.

Revision

Reporting an error message problem

Each InfoTool message has an identifier. Message identifiers that begin with ABU indicate programming errors that you can probably correct without help from a service representative. For information about ABU messages and how to correct the errors, see *InfoTool Programming Reference*.

When you receive an error message, follow these steps:

1. Check the third letter of the message identifier. If the letter is U (as in ABU1114E), see Step 2. If the letter is S (as in ABS1225E), see Step 3.

2. If the third letter is U, you can probably fix the problem yourself. For help with a particular message, see *InfoTool Programming Reference*, which lists all InfoTool messages.

3. If the third letter is S, call 1-800-555-1111 and tell the representative the message identifier. The representative will work with you to resolve the problem quickly.

This previous passage points out a challenge that writers sometimes face. When the product you are writing about is hard to use, it's sometimes very difficult to make using that product seem easy. In this case, the writer's job would have been much easier if the descriptions of all or most of the product's error messages included actions that the user could take. Forcing users to call a service representative for 150 error situations is far from ideal, but the products for which technical writers provide information aren't always ideal.

Writing about a difficult-to-use product is both a challenge and an opportunity for you as a writer. When you write about a product that is difficult to use, work with the product designers or programmers to improve the usability of the product. Usability testing can be helpful here, as it is in many other writing situations.

Cover each topic in just as much detail as users need

Including a topic doesn't necessarily mean that you have covered it adequately. The goal should be to include enough detail for users to perform their tasks, but no more detail than they need. While you're analyzing tasks, you might not be able to anticipate all the details of a task; later, when you're writing, questions of detail will arise. Judgments about the completeness of detail are usually more subjective than judgments about the completeness of topics. However, writers who "put themselves in their users' shoes" can usually make good decisions about how much detail is needed.

To understand what information is needed, you must know something about your audience. For example, are your users experienced or inexperienced with your product? with similar products? Knowing the experience level of your audience helps you determine what information is relevant.

Writing about a product is easiest when your audience is homogeneous— either all experienced or all inexperienced. On one hand, if your information is about a new product, you can assume your audience is made up of novices, at least with this product. On the other hand, if your information is about a well-established product that has been on the market for a long time with few new users, you can assume that most of your audience is experienced.

The challenge that writers frequently face is to successfully handle a mix of experience levels. You don't want to bog down the experienced user with lots of introductory information. However, you also don't want to make assumptions that cause major problems for novice users, as in the following example.

Original

> **To build InfoTool files:**
>   1. Log in to the control point host or managed host as root.
>   2. Change to the directory containing the driver build script.
>   3. Run the driver build script.
>   4. Change to the directory containing the watchdog build script.
>   5. Run the watchdog build script.

To build InfoTool files:

1. Log in to the control point host or managed host as root.
2. Change to the directory containing the driver build script. For example:

   cd `infotool_path/system_dir/drivers/inft64/obj`

3. Run the driver build script.

   build_inft_drv

4. Change to the directory containing the watchdog build script.
5. Run the watchdog build script.

   build_inft_wdog

   You now have the required files for InfoTool operations on workstations using the same operating system as the current workstation.

The writer of the original passage assumed that users knew all the commands and object names that are necessary to follow the procedure. In some cases, this assumption might be valid, such as when your audience is experienced. In the revised passage, the writer has included necessary detail for less experienced users who don't know the commands and object names but still need to follow the procedure.

If your audience is a mix of experience levels, you need to make decisions about how to satisfy all their information needs, without causing problems for either group. Some approaches you might select are to:

❏ Write both online and printed information primarily to an experienced audience, but provide extensive online help to assist novices.

❏ Put the information into two separate forms, such as advanced topics for experienced users and a tutorial for novices.

❏ Integrate the information within one online or printed document, but separate the introductory from advanced topics (such as in different windows, chapters, or parts).

❏ Integrate the information, but graphically distinguish between information for different experience levels.

An example of this last approach is seen in books that separate the technical detail for the experts into boxes, sometimes called *sidebars*, with special graphical icons to attract users' attention.

Include enough information

When developing information, or when you're editing information you or others have written, look for logical holes, areas where some information might be missing. Some types of information are vulnerable to problems of incompleteness.

Information about conditions. If you mention or explain one of multiple conditions, mention or explain all the conditions. Otherwise, your user is left wondering about the other conditions. For example, when you describe events with words such as "usually" or "normally," users might wonder what happens when the unusual or abnormal occurs. Mention not only common occurrences, but also the uncommon ones, especially if users need special information to handle the situation.

For example, the writer of the revised passage on page 56 could add information about what to do if the build process fails (in steps and), such as: "If the build fails, you'll receive an error message. Refer to the online Message Help for information about how to deal with the problem."

Procedures. When you write user instructions, follow every possible path in the procedure. For a complex procedure with many possible paths, you might use a graphic to help orient users. The more decision points in a procedure, the more helpful a graphic is likely to be. For example, the revised passage on page 54 might be enhanced by a graphic like this:

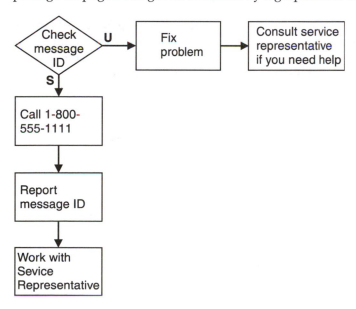

Citations. When you refer users to other information, be it online or printed, ask yourself "What does a user need to know when deciding whether to pursue this information?" Don't merely give a title; indicate why you think the source is worth investigating. For example, instead of saying, "See *InfoBase User's Guide*," say, "For information about using InfoBase's indexing function, see *InfoBase User's Guide*."

Rather than including an actual heading from another source, use descriptive words that are likely to remain in the index even if the heading changes from one edition to the next. (Using descriptive words when you refer to other information also helps you validate the accuracy of citations when you update your information in future editions.) Don't expect the user to read the entire referenced source just to figure out why you thought that information might be helpful.

When you use a hypertext link in an online document or Web page, and when the text of the link is part of a sentence, make sure to include in the link the words that indicate the type of information to which the link takes the user.

For example, if your link takes the user to information on creating an infowidget, make the link's text **create an infowidget**, rather than **infowidget**. If only the noun, infowidget, is included in the link, the user will probably assume the linked-to information defines the term rather than explains how to create one.

Detailed syntax. When documenting the syntax of commands, calls, statements, or macros, ask yourself, "How much detail does the programmer really need?" For example, if you are explaining the graphical technique you use for showing command syntax to your audience of programmers, your explanation should cover every element of that syntax, even the one-character keyword separators.

Regardless of the situation, try to identify and provide the level of detail your audience needs.

Include only necessary information

Too much information also creates problems of completeness. Unnecessary detail slows down the user, making it more difficult to find and use needed information.

Introductions to topics frequently contain more detail than users need, as in the following passage.

Original

Find the Tab key in the upper left area of your keyboard.

Try pressing this key. It moves the cursor between the two input fields.

In the User ID input field, type: `tailor`

Find the Backspace key in the upper right corner of the alphanumeric area.

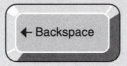

Try pressing this key. It erases by going backward from where the cursor is.

You can also erase characters by pressing the long key, called the Space bar, at the bottom of the keyboard. However, the Space bar erases by going forward from where the cursor is.

The original passage includes too many details, both text and graphical elements, on how to use a standard keyboard. Unless this is a product that teaches a user how to type, this detail is extraneous. The following revised passage tells users what keys they generally use to enter data on the input window, but it excludes unnecessary detail.

Revision

When you enter data on the input window, the primary keys you use are the letter keys, number keys, Tab key, Space bar, and Backspace key.

Use the Tab key to move from one input field on the window to another.

If you make a mistake when entering data, erase it by using the Backspace key or Space bar.

Too much detail is frequently the result of writing to more than one type of user or to no particular user at all. Sometimes the writer includes extra detail for secondary users, which can distract primary users.

In this section, the terms *primary user* and *secondary user* refer to your audience—the users of your information—not to users of the product. If you are writing a tutorial, your audience doesn't include experienced product users. Likewise, if your information covers advanced topics exclusively, your audience doesn't include novice users. Typically, if you make these distinctions, you do so as you analyze your audience and related requirements when you design your information.

Ask yourself: How important are the secondary users? Will they really be in the audience? How (and how much) do they differ from the primary audience? Can the information they need be omitted or put elsewhere?

In the following example, assume that most users of the product will use the graphical interface and associated online help, but the majority of the readers of the printed information (your primary users) will use the text-based installation program.

Original

> **Configuring an InfoInstaller Control Point**
>
> To configure an InfoInstaller control point, you can use either the graphical program (Infinstg) or the text-only program (Infinsty). If you use the graphical program, you must have installed InfoFinder.
>
> Preparing to Configure a Control Point
>
> Before configuring an InfoInstaller control point, you need to:
>
> 1. Determine (or create) the InfoInstaller control database. If you are using Infinstg, click mouse button 2 on the CDB icon to see the name of the control database. If no CDB icon is on your desktop, you need to create the database. If you are using Infinsty, go to a command line and enter:
>
>    ```
>    create infinsty database
>    ```
>
>   If this database already exists, you will receive an error message.
>
> 2. *and so on*

In the original passage (in which only one of the necessary steps is shown), the first step addresses both primary users (who use Infinsty) and secondary users (who use Infinstg), even though:

❑ The actions these users take differ.
❑ The procedure for Infinstg users is available as part of the graphical interface.

The following revised passage shows that two separate procedures have been created. The primary users (of this printed information) need not be burdened by information directed at the secondary users. And the secondary users (of the printed information) can access the information they need while they are using the graphical interface.

Revision

Configuring an InfoInstaller Control Point

To configure an InfoInstaller control point, you can use either the graphical program (Infinstg) or the text-only program (Infinsty). If you use the graphical program, you must have installed InfoFinder.

To use the graphical program, double-click the Infinstg icon on your desktop, and follow the online directions.

If you are using the text-only program, you must do some preparation before proceeding with the configuration.

Preparing to Configure a Control Point

1. At a command line, enter:

   ```
   create infinsty database
   ```

2. *and so on*

Use patterns of information to ensure proper coverage

As previous sections have shown, you can eliminate extraneous information and identify redundancies by analyzing user tasks and by using and testing the information. Another way to determine whether you have covered all the relevant topics and details is to develop a *pattern* for structuring your information. Patterns help users become comfortable with the organization of information and focus on the content they need.

A pattern is an organizational device that you can use to make information consistent. Therefore, this guideline is similar to "Organize information consistently" on page 146 in the chapter on organization.

A good way to develop a pattern is to start with the question: "What does a user need to know to perform the task?" From the answer, you can define a pattern of the information such as:

Definition
Main task
Subtasks
Related tasks
Definition of interface fields and buttons

For online information, help windows for similar topics should contain the same types of help information in the same level of detail. If contextual help is available on some fields, it should be available on all fields. If a help window includes a summary list of tasks with links to more information, similar summaries should also have links, as in the following pair of help windows.

Original

Help

Use this object to access an SQL table.
An SQL table represents a table in a database.
When you open the object, you see all the data in the table.

Using this object, you can:

- ☐ **Create an SQL table**
- ☐ **View and change data in an SQL table or SQL view**
- ☐ **Delete an SQL table or SQL view**
- ☐ **Create a shadow**

You cannot copy an SQL table.

Help

Use this object to access authorization information about an SQL table.

Using this object, you can:

- ☐ Grant authority to users
- ☐ Revoke authority to users
- ☐ Query the authorization level of users

In the original pair of help windows, the first window uses links and the second does not.

The following revised pair of help windows demonstrates the pattern of using links for a task summary.

Revision

Help ▢▢▢

Use this object to access an SQL table.
An SQL table represents a table in a database.
When you open the object, you see all the data in the table.

Using this object, you can:

❏ **Create an SQL table**
❏ **View and change data in an SQL table or SQL view**
❏ **Delete an SQL table or SQL view**
❏ **Create a shadow**

You cannot copy an SQL table.

Help ▢▢▢

Use this object to access authorization information about an SQL table.

Using this object, you can:

❏ **Grant authority to users**
❏ **Revoke authority to users**
❏ **Query the authorization level of users**

Patterns are also useful for explaining how to perform a task. Guidance information about a task that is standard from one product or environment to another, such as installation, might have many of the same subtasks in common.

In the following passage, assume that InfoBase and InfoTool are companion products that run in the same operating environment and are installed the same way.

Original

> **Installing InfoBase**
>
> To install InfoBase:
>
> 1. Review hardware and software prerequisites.
> 2. Install the InfoBase program files.
> 3. Configure the InfoBase environment.
> 4. Verify the installation and configuration.
>
> **
>
> **Installing InfoTool**
>
> To install InfoTool:
>
> 1. Review hardware and software prerequisites.
> 2. Identify prerequisites that aren't installed and install them.
> 3. Install the InfoTool program files.
> 4. Configure the InfoTool environment.
> 5. <u>Verify the installation and configuration.</u>

In the original passage, the overviews of the installation task for InfoBase and InfoTool differ in that the first overview omits the step of installing prerequisite products before installing the program.

The writer of the following revised passage has used a pattern to ensure that both sections contain the same kind of information, in the same sequence, and in the same level of detail. Users who install both programs can be confident that all the relevant information is present.

Revision

Installing InfoBase

To install InfoBase:

1. Review hardware and software prerequisites.
2. Identify prerequisites that aren't installed and install them.
3. Install the InfoBase program files.
4. Configure the InfoBase environment.
5. Verify the installation and configuration.

****

Installing InfoTool

To install InfoTool:

1. Review hardware and software prerequisites.
2. Identify prerequisites that aren't installed and install them.
3. Install the InfoTool program files.
4. Configure the InfoTool environment.
5. <u>Verify the installation and configuration.</u>

When using patterns to ensure completeness, however, you need to make sure the pattern you use is correct. If the writer of the previous help windows had used the InfoBase structure as the pattern for InfoTool help windows, the necessary information about installing prerequisite products would have been missing from the installation instructions for both InfoBase and InfoTool. Before using a given information pattern for other information, verify that the pattern is valid by collecting user feedback or performing usability testing.

As in guidance information, patterns in reference information are very useful. A structured type of pattern, a template, is useful for ensuring that all standard parts of parallel, or similar, topics are included. A template is like a cookie cutter, which is good for replicating a standard object in a consistent way.

Original

```
Statements
ALTER
   Syntax
   Examples
   Usage Notes
BACKUP
   Usage Notes
CHANGE
   Syntax
   Examples
   Usage Notes
```

Revision

```
Statements
ALTER
   Syntax
   Examples
   Usage Notes
BACKUP
   Syntax
   Examples
   Usage Notes
CHANGE
   Syntax
   Examples
   Usage Notes
```

In the original table of contents, the section on the BACKUP statement doesn't have some important information—syntax and examples. The revised table of contents includes these pieces of information. Using a pattern or template for reference information can help you ensure you've covered all similar topics in the same level of detail.

Repeat information only when users will benefit from it

Repetition can be good or bad. Needless repetition is bad; it is extraneous detail that wastes reading time and might give a wrong impression about what is important. Repetition is good when it appropriately emphasizes and reinforces important points or enables users to avoid an unnecessary branch to another page.

Original

> To select a different set of fonts, change your directory to *fonts*, and copy the font file you want to use to your printer. For information about how to change a directory, see *InfoWrite Operations Guide*. For information about copying files, see *InfoWrite Command Reference*. For information about the font files that are available to you, see *InfoWrite Quick Reference*.

Revision

> To select a different set of fonts, follow these steps:
>
> 1. Change your directory to *fonts*.
>
>    ```
>    cd\fonts
>    ```
>
> 2. Review the following list of available font files and decide which one best meets your needs:
>
>   Arial
>   Brittanica
>   Courier
>   Engravers
>   Futura
>   Hogbold
>   Times New Roman
>
> 3. Copy the font file you want to use to your printer.
>
>    ```
>    copy filename.fnt lpt1
>    ```

In the original passage, the user must hunt for as many as three separate books and then, after these books are located, hunt again for the specific information in each. It's true that you wouldn't want to copy everything that might be found in another information source. However, to send the user to different sources for information about a simple instruction (such as copy or change directory) or for a short list of available fonts seems unnecessary. The revised passage includes the necessary detail in one place and doesn't force the user to go to other sources.

When you repeat information unnecessarily, you not only interrupt and delay the user's task, but you might also confuse a user and waste space—especially online space.

Original

> **Help**
>
> Finding an object
>
> 1. Point to a folder object or an empty area on the desktop.
>   A folder is a container used to organize objects, programs, documents, other folders, or any combination of these.
> 2. Click mouse button 2, which is on the right side of the mouse.
> 3. Select **Find**. This choice will help you locate the object you want.
> 4. Type the name of the object you want to find in the **Name** field. Type * if you don't know the name. An asterisk tells the system to look for all names.
> 5. Select the type of object you are looking for.
> 6. and so on

Revision

> **Help**
>
> Finding an object
>
> 1. Point to a folder object or an empty area on the desktop.
> 2. Click mouse button 2.
> 3. Select **Find**.
> 4. Type the name of the object you want to find in the **Name** field. Type * if you don't know the name.
> 5. Select the type of object you are looking for.
> 6. and so on

In the original help window, steps through repeat details that are covered by other contextual help windows, making this procedure longer than necessary (possibly forcing the user to scroll). The revised help window provides only the information appropriate for this task.

In sum

Use the guidelines in this chapter to ensure that technical information contains the appropriate amount of information for your audience (enough information without being overly complete). Refer to the examples in the chapter for practical applications of these guidelines.

When you review technical information for completeness, you can use this checklist in two ways:

❏ As a reminder of what to look for, to ensure a thorough review
❏ As an evaluation tool, to determine the quality of the information

You can apply the quality rating in the third column of the checklist to the guideline as a whole. Judging by the number and severity of items you found, decide how the information rates on each guideline for this quality characteristic. You can then add your findings to "Quality Checklist" on page 269, which covers all the quality characteristics.

Although the guidelines are intended to cover all areas for this quality characteristic, you might find additional items to add to the list for a guideline.

Guidelines for completeness	Items to look for	Quality rating
Cover all topics that support users' tasks, and only those topics.	• Information contains no extraneous topics such as product internals. • Topics the user needs for performing tasks are covered. • An appropriate amount of introductory information is included for the audience. • Information that doesn't directly support a user task explains why a user needs it.	1 2 3 4 5
Cover each topic in just as much detail as users need.	• Explanations contain enough detail. • Procedures for a user task are complete; no steps are missing. • Syntax rules are complete. • All syntax elements are described. • Secondary topics are described in less detail than primary topics. • Only the most common uses are described in detail. • New concepts are sufficiently developed. • References to related information are meaningful. • Introductory information is sufficiently detailed for the audience.	1 2 3 4 5
Use patterns of information to ensure proper coverage.	• Parallel pieces of information are explained in a similar level of detail. • Standard parts are included. • Promised information is included.	1 2 3 4 5
Repeat information only when users will benefit from it.	• Information that is repeated is important to the user, who would be troubled by looking in another section or book. • Information has no unnecessarily repeated sections.	1 2 3 4 5

Note: The scale for the quality rating goes from very satisfied (1) to very dissatisfied (5).

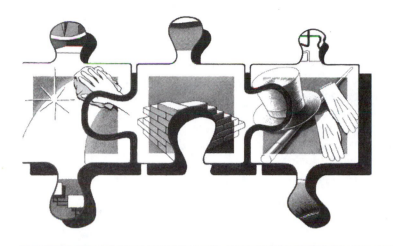

Part 2

Easy to Understand

Whether technical information is easy to understand depends on how it is presented at the level of small structures such as words and sentences. It can also involve larger structures such as examples and scenarios.

Chapter 5

Clarity

Clear information is information that users can understand the first time. They don't have to reread it to untangle grammatical connections, sort out excess words, decipher ambiguities, figure out relationships, or interpret the meaning. Clarity in technical information is like a window that opens to the subject.

For most writers, words don't tumble out clearly the first time that they try to write about something. Often, to break through a block, writers write as if they were speaking, but that introduces problems such as unnecessary words, vague referents, and rambling sentences. People can get visual and auditory cues when you're speaking, but written words are on their own for conveying a message.

Clear information is mainly the result of rewriting—replacing, adding, and deleting parts to achieve clarity. Clear information requires close attention to each word, phrase, sentence, and other elements to make sure that each participates appropriately in the message. This attention is probably more helpful when you are rewriting than when you are first writing.

Clarity provides the rationale for many decisions about style and for some decisions about visual effectiveness. You might choose, for example, bold-face for certain kinds of words and italics for certain other kinds; consistently applying these style decisions enhances clarity by making information easier for users to understand the first time.

Aspects of clarity also overlap aspects of completeness (especially too much information and relevance) and organization (especially consistency and subordination). Clear information requires a strong focus on what users need to know and when they need to know it. Extraneous information muddies the message. Relationships among pieces of information (whether in sentences, lists, tables, or some other format) must be clear.

To make information clear, follow these guidelines:

❏ **Focus on the meaning.**

❏ **Avoid ambiguity.**

❏ **Keep elements short.**

❏ **Write cohesively.**

❏ **Present similar topics in a similar way.**

❏ **Use technical terms only if they are necessary and appropriate.**

❏ **Define each term that is new to the intended audience.**

Focus on the meaning

Clear information requires that you focus on what you want to say. What's the point? What do you want the users to do or know?

When most people write, they need to warm up to a subject. They need to write a while before the words flow and they see what they need to say. A first pass can produce long sentences, imprecise words, unnecessary modifiers, and rambling paragraphs.

The following paragraph gives an overview of a product for storing and retrieving image data.

Original

> A major company maintains a large personnel database that it basically makes use of for many kinds of employee-related applications such as payroll and benefits. The company now has some plans to extend the database significantly to include current pictures of employees and use the pictures as the basis for a very modern security system. The system is specifically designed to protect secure areas of the company's building from access by any people who really do not have authorization to be there.

Each sentence has over 25 words, but are they all needed? Does each contribute to the meaning? In an inflated economy people have to spend lots of money for just a loaf of bread; in this "inflated" passage users have to read many more words than the message warrants.

Contributors to the "wordflation" in this paragraph are:

Imprecise words

"now has plans to," "makes use of," "kinds of"

Intensifying words

"basically," "significantly," "very," "specifically," "really," "some," "any"

When you revise the passage to remove these, you get:

First Revision

> A major company maintains a large personnel database that it uses for many employee-related applications such as payroll and benefits. The company plans to extend the database to include current pictures of employees and use the pictures as the basis for a modern security system. The system is designed to protect secure areas of the company's building from access by people who do not have authorization to be there.

This revision is clearer, but the passage is still not as clear as it could be. There is a problem with the modifiers. The writer modified many nouns, but only a few modifiers are needed:

- ❏ "Major" and "large" do not supply useful information in this situation; in fact, they detract by limiting the example unnecessarily. Unfortunately, the emphasis in the first part of the sentence falls on them, as you will find if you read the sentence aloud.

- ❏ You don't need "many" as a modifier of the applications if you also have the examples of applications.

- ❏ "Current" is not needed because in this context you can take for granted that the pictures should be up to date.

- ❏ "Modern" introduces a judgment that is probably not needed in a paragraph that is not intended for marketing the product.

- ❏ "Secure" as a modifier of "areas" is confusing because the areas won't be secure unless they are protected.

- ❏ "Company's" is superfluous because the context should make clear that the building is the one associated with the company.

- ❏ The modifier of "access" is a long phrase that you can shorten just to "unauthorized."

When you remove the unnecessary modifiers, you get:

Second Revision

> A company maintains a personnel database that it uses for employee-related applications such as payroll and benefits. The company plans to extend the database to include pictures of employees and use the pictures as the basis for a security system. The system is designed to protect certain areas of the building from unauthorized access.

By focusing imprecise words and removing intensifying words and unnecessary modifiers, you reduced the length of the sentences by around a third. Now the meaning is clearer, but you can make it clearer by removing extraneous information. In this context users care about the company's extending the database for image data but not about the company's maintaining the database or using it for many employee-related applications. The writer has used the first sentence to ease into the subject, but the sentence is not needed for clarity.

Third Revision

> A company plans to extend its personnel database to include employee pictures. The company wants to use the pictures in a security system that will protect certain areas of the building from unauthorized access.

The revised paragraph focuses on the company and the relationship between the personnel database, employee pictures, and the security system.

The revised paragraph now has only two sentences. You might find that there is more you want to say in this paragraph. Perhaps, you could mention the product as a way of storing and retrieving the pictures in the database.

Some writers believe that a good paragraph should have at least three sentences—one that introduces the topic, one that develops the topic, and one that summarizes the additional information and leads into a new topic. Such a formula for a paragraph can help you think through a topic. However, the formula should not result in extra sentences that get in the way of the message. Clarity is better served by a short paragraph than by one with extra sentences, especially as the topic sentence.

When you focus on what you want to say, you can fix many clarity problems, especially:

❑ Imprecise verbs
❑ Overuse of intensifying words
❑ Long sentences
❑ Unnecessary modifiers
❑ Rambling paragraphs

For lists of imprecise and precise verbs and intensifying words, see "Words to Watch for Clarity" on page 281.

Avoid ambiguity

This guideline could be called "Have mercy on translators and non-native speakers." These people are more likely than native speakers to have difficulty when writing is ambiguous.

Choose and use words with a clear meaning

Words that have more than one meaning can be confusing, particularly when more than one meaning fits the context. Some ambiguous words are small but important in conveying information about relationships between clauses:

Problems arise when words such as *since*, *once*, *as*, and *while* could indicate either time or something else, such as cause or contrast. For example:

Original

> Since you created the table, you have authority to change the table.

Revision

> Because you created the table, you have authority to change the table.

A native speaker would probably recognize that "since" in the original passage applies to cause rather than time. However, it's better to use the unambiguous word than to rely on the context to help users make the right choice.

Because of the richness of the English language, the words you choose will probably have more than one meaning. However, you can reduce the confusion over which meaning a word has in a particular context by using the word consistently with only one of its meanings. For example, use "replace the part" to mean only "put the part back" and not also "substitute a new part for the one you have."

May and *can* are confusing when they are used interchangeably in technical information. As a child, you probably learned to use *may* when asking for permission. In technical information, *may* rarely has the meaning of permission but is sometimes used ambiguously to indicate possibility or capability, as in the following sentence:

```
You may restrict authority to issue certain commands.
```

Does this sentence mean that the user can restrict the use of the commands or that the user might do so from time to time? It's impossible to know, unless the surrounding information uses *may* and *can* conscientiously, preparing the user for the intended meaning here.

Do not use *may* and *can* interchangeably. Reserve *may* for the possibility of doing something and *can* for the ability or power to do it. In technical information, it's probably more often appropriate to talk about capability than possibility.

Might indicates a greater degree of uncertainty about a possibility and so indicates possibility less ambiguously than *may* does. You could choose to use *might* rather than *may* in many sentences dealing with possibility.

For a list of words that can be hard to translate, see "Words to Watch for Clarity" on page 281.

Avoid vague referents

Another clarity problem for translators and non-native speakers is vague referents. Sometimes when writers use a pronoun to refer to a noun, the noun is vague for any of these reasons:

❑ It is far from the pronoun, perhaps in another sentence.
❑ It is among other nouns that might fit as the one being referred to.
❑ It is not stated explicitly.

Consider these examples of vague referents:

Original

> InfoGrammar is a virtual database that you can create from the target file system. It consists of a set of statements that provide input to the projection utility.

Revision

> InfoGrammar is a virtual database that you can create from the target file system. This database consists of a set of statements that provide input to the projection utility.

Clarity

The original passage is confusing because you're not sure whether "it" refers to InfoGrammar or the target file system. Is the referent the closer noun or the earlier subject? The revision specifies "database," clarifying the referent without repeating it.

Original

> You can have multiple catalogs for a single source; however, each can access only one.

Revision

> You can have multiple catalogs for a single source; however, each catalog can access only one source.

In the original passage. the referents for "each" and "one" are not clear. Native speakers might guess the right referents, aided by the order of the nouns in the first clause, but it takes time to consider whether "each source can access only one catalog" might be meant.

A pronoun such as *it*, *this*, or *that* at the start of a sentence can cause confusion, as in the following passage.

Original

> Copy this file so that you can edit and save your version locally. This is especially important when InfoProduct is installed on a network and you want to run a customized version of the product.

Revision

> Copy this file so that you can edit and save your version locally. Having your own copy is especially important when InfoProduct is installed on a network and you want to run a customized version of the product.

The original passage refers to a noun that is only implied in the preceding sentence. The revised passage replaces the pronoun with a noun.

Place modifiers appropriately

Modifiers that are placed inappropriately cause confusion, as in the following sentence.

Original

> Click the configuration server that you want to link the list manager servers to in the Configure Server Name field.

The phrase "in the Configure Server Name field" is out of place. That field is not where the linking occurs. It is where the names of the configuration servers are, and so you might revise this passage as:

First Revision

> Click the name of the configuration server in the Configuration Server Name field that you want to link the list manager servers to.

Now you have another problem of a misplaced modifier. The *that* clause should modify "configuration server" and not the field, which it is next to. You have two choices, as in the following revision.

Second Revision

> Click the name (in the Configuration Server Name field) of the configuration server that you want to link the list manager servers to.
>
> In the Configuration Server Name field, click the name of the configuration server that you want to link the list manager servers to.

Depending on the context, you could choose to set off the intervening phrase or to give the position first and then specify the action.

Only is probably the biggest source of ambiguity because it can modify almost any kind of word and so can occur in almost any position in a sentence. For clarity, put *only* immediately before the word or words that it modifies.

Original

> The grid is only active when an object is placed or dragged on a form.

Revision

> The grid is active only when an object is placed or dragged on a form.

The revision moves *only* to the position where it emphasizes the conditions under which the grid is active.

Avoid long strings of nouns

Unlike languages where nouns have a gender, English lets you use nouns as adjectives. The names of software or hardware features and functions seem particularly prone to couplings of nouns, such as "work load," "table space," "error message," "access key," and "procedure call.," Over time some pairs become accepted as one word, as in "database" and "workstation."

Also common as names of features and functions are strings of three nouns, such as "program request handler," "attribute properties window," and "network terminal option." These combinations can cause confusion about what modifies what. For example, is the handler for program requests, or is the request handler for programs? Does the middle noun go with the first noun or the last noun, or are the three equal?

If the first pair of nouns in a threesome serves as an adjective for the third noun, consider using a hyphen, as in "character-set identifier." The threesome should not be well established as having no hyphen.

Do not use a noun string to modify another noun string. The buildup of nouns can quickly become confusing, as in the following sentence.

Original

> Use the input message destination transaction code as shown in the example.

Revision

> Use the transaction code for the destination of an input message as shown in the example.

The original passage makes it difficult to determine whether "destination" goes with the first pair or the second pair of nouns. To make sense of a long string of nouns, insert prepositions and articles.

Be careful when using adjectives with a string of two or three nouns. Because English uses placement to determine what modifies what, it's sometimes hard to know whether an adjective modifies one of the nouns or the set, as in the following sentence.

Original

> The sample dynamic plan selection user exit is in Appendix B.

First Revision

> The sample user exit for dynamic plan selection is in Appendix B.

The revised passage sorts out what modifies what by placing the first adjective with the last noun pair. However, the noun pair "plan selection" is a poor twosome because it masks a verb, as shown in the following revision.

Second Revision

> The sample user exit for dynamically selecting a plan is in Appendix B.

Avoid creating noun strings with nouns that should be verbs. "Performance control" and "error recovery" are other examples of such nouns.

Consider changing any strings with more than two nouns. When unpacking a long noun string, start with the noun or pair of nouns at the end.

You may be stuck with some noun strings because of existing terminology in a field or in your product. However, be careful not to create new ones, especially ones where a verb should be used instead.

Write positively

More than one negative word in a sentence can make the sentence more difficult to understand. If you put two negative words (such as "not unlike") in a clause, you make the clause positive. Research shows that readers have more trouble understanding a sentence that has double negatives than an equivalent positive sentence.

The main negative words to be concerned about are *no, not, none, never,* and *nothing.* Consider the following sentence.

Original

> Do not install InfoConnect until you check that your computer does not have these conflicting programs.

First Revision

> Before you install InfoConnect, check that your computer does not have these conflicting programs.

The original sentence is difficult because of the negatives in two clauses. The revision changes the negative "not...until" in the main clause to a positive form, making the negative in the dependent clause easier to understand. Telling users what to do is much stronger than only implying it by saying what not to do.

Some negatives mask a need to supply more information.

Second Revision

> Before you install InfoConnect, check your computer for these conflicting programs.

This revision gets rid of the negative "does not have" and prepares the way for information about what to do if you do find the conflicting programs on your computer.

If you can state a sentence in positive terms, do so.

Original

> Transitions cannot occur between states that are inherited from different classes or between local and inherited states.

Revision

> Transitions can occur only between states that are inherited from the same class or between states that are defined in the object.

The revision gives the same information but avoids the negative. This positive approach is particularly important for a sentence that starts a paragraph.

For a list of negative expressions, see "Words to Watch for Clarity" on page 281.

Clarity

Keep elements short

Wordiness wastes reading time, online space, and paper, and sometimes buries the message. As you saw in the section "Focus on the meaning," extra words can get in the way, making users sort through the words to weed out the excess. This section presents more ways to get rid of extra words.

Remove roundabout expressions and needless repetition

Roundabout expressions use several words where one or two or none will do. In speaking, people often use extra words to gain time to think about the next thing to say. In writing, however, these extra words are like noise and hamper the meaning.

Original

> Given the fact that you have created an object, it can operate in a manner independent of other objects based on the same class.

Revision

> After you create an object, it can operate independently of other objects of the same class.

The original sentence uses several roundabout expressions. They tend to crop up when you want to connect important parts of a sentence, as if a simple preposition or conjunction were not enough.

Using repetitive words such as "subject matter" is a habit in English that started when people wanted to show that they knew how to say something in more than one language. They would combine an Anglo-Saxon word such as *new* with the Latinate word such as *innovation*.

People still carry on this habit of needless repetition, as in the following sentence.

Original

> You can display a visible grid on forms to help you place components.

88

Developing Quality Technical Information

Revision

> You can display a grid on forms to help you place components.

If you're displaying the grid, presumably it is visible. The revision removes the needless repetition.

For lists of roundabout and repetitive words, see "Words to Watch for Clarity" on page 281.

Choose direct words

In addition to choosing between using more words and using fewer words, you have a choice when two words have much the same meaning. Sometimes English has a word that derives from Latin (such as *assist*) and a word that derives from Anglo-Saxon (such as *help*) for the same thing. In these cases, the Anglo-Saxon word is usually shorter and more direct, as in the following sentence.

Original

> Modifications to a shared property apply universally to objects on the object list.

Revision

> Changes to a shared property apply to all objects on the object list.

As with intensifying words, you might sometimes decide to use a Latin-derived word. Such a word will be more effective because of its rarity. For lists of these pairs of words, see "Words to Watch for Clarity" on page 281.

As you will see in "Use appropriate and consistent tone" in the chapter on style, your choice of words affects the tone of what you write.

Keep lists short

Long lists of items, especially subtasks, can overwhelm users. Users tend to feel more optimistic about succeeding at a task if the subtasks do not run on and on. They need to comprehend the task as a whole and see how the parts contribute to it.

When users need to remember the items in a list, be particularly careful to keep lists short:

❑ Seven items maximum for online information
❑ Nine items maximum for printed information

If a group of items in a list exceeds these limits, create smaller groups, as in the following pair of examples.

Original

To create a pop-up menu:

1. Click a new form.

2. Choose **Selected->Open menu** in the Project window.

3. In the Menu Editor window, choose **Selected->Add item**.

4. Choose **Selected->Add subitem**.

5. Choose **Selected->Add subitem**.

   You will get a `Menu1` menu with commands `Menu2` and `Menu3`.

6. Double-click `Menu1` to open the Property Editor, and set the Visible property to False.

7. Also in the Property Editor, change the Name property to pMenu.

8. Choose **Selected->Code** in the Project window to open the Code Editor.

9. In the Code Editor, select the Form object and the Mouse_Up event.

10. Enter the following code, which calls the PopupMenu method with the name you gave the invisible menu on the menu bar:

```
Sub Form_MouseUp(Button As Integer, Shift As Integer,      X
As Single, Y As Single)
If Button=2, Then  'Right mouse button?
PopupMenu pMenu 'Call method

End If
End Sub
```

11. Run the application. Click the form with mouse button 2, and choose one of the commands displayed by the PopupMenu method.

    The pop-up menu opens; it closes after you choose the command.

This list of 11 items is too long, and some items are confusing. The procedure involves several windows and editors. Grouping the steps around more general tasks clarifies the procedure.

Revision

To create a pop-up menu:

1. Click a new form to open the Project window.

2. In the Project window, choose **Selected->Open menu** to open the Menu Editor.

3. Edit the menus. In the Menu Editor:

   a. Choose **Selected->Add item**.

   b. Choose **Selected->Add subitem** two times.

   You will get a `Menu1` menu with commands `Menu2` and `Menu3`.

   c. Double-click `Menu1` to open the Property Editor.

4. Edit the properties. In the Property Editor:

   a. Set the Visible property to False.

   b. Change the Name property to pMenu.

5. Edit the code. In the Project window, choose **Selected->Code** to open the Code Editor. In the Code Editor:

   a. Select the Form object and the Mouse_Up event.

   b. Enter the following code, which calls the PopupMenu method with the name you gave the invisible menu on the menu bar:

```
Sub Form_MouseUp(Button As Integer, Shift As Integer,          X
As Single, Y As Single)
If Button=2, Then   'Right mouse button?
PopupMenu pMenu   'Call method
End If
End Sub
```

6. Run the application. Click the form with mouse button 2, and choose one of the commands displayed by the PopupMenu method.

   The pop-up menu opens; it closes after you choose the command.

With the grouping of steps by more general tasks, the number of steps has decreased from 11 to six. In the revision, the first two steps are clearly just for navigation and the middle three steps are clearly the heart of the procedure.

Lists of reference information (often presented in alphabetical order) can be acceptable if longer because they are for looking up rather than for reading from beginning to end.

Write cohesively

Elements such as sentences, lists, tables, figures, and examples that are clear on their own do not necessarily add up to clarity overall. These elements must work together to emphasize the most important ideas that you want to convey. The ideas expressed in each element should not have equal weight. Instead, some should reinforce others, contributing to the overall impact.

Make explicit the logical flow from idea to idea. This flow can take many forms, such as from sentence to sentence, from paragraph to paragraph, from a paragraph to a list, table, figure, or example and back again.

You can use transitional words at the start of sentences such as "for example," "therefore," and "as a result." To integrate lists, tables, figures, or examples, you can introduce them with a phrase or sentence and provide meaningful captions for tables and figures, as in the following passage.

Original

> A grid is a set of horizontal and vertical lines that appear on InfoProduct forms. A grid is active only when objects are placed or moved on forms.
>
> You can display a grid on forms to help you place components. You can control the size and visibility of the grid lines. The grid is useful when you draw or place components as they are created or when you move and resize them.
>
> If you want the grid lines to be visible, set the Visible property to True. To change the space between grid lines, type new values in the Height and Width fields. These values measure the distance in twips (a Twentieth of an Inch Point) between the grid lines
>
> | Property | Possible Values | Default | Effect |
> |---|---|---|---|
> | Active | True
False | True | Makes an object align with the grid lines
Lets you place an object anywhere on the form |
> | Size | 45 to 1485 twips | 5 pixels | Size.Width=Int sets the vertical space between lines
Size.Height=Int sets the horizontal space between lines |
> | Visible | True
False | True | Makes the grid visible
Makes the grid invisible |

Taken individually, each sentence is clear. However, the paragraphs are not clear, and the table is not integrated. Judging by the first sentence in each paragraph, you can surmise that the first paragraph describes a grid, the second paragraph tells what you can do with a grid, and the third paragraph tells how to use the properties. Looking more closely at the sentences, however, you find that the flow of ideas is:

❏ Paragraph 1
  — Definition of grid
  — Restriction on when the grid is available

❏ Paragraph 2
  — Usefulness of a grid
  — Aspects of a grid that you can customize
  — Usefulness of a grid

❏ Paragraph 3
  — How to make grid lines visible
  — How to change the space between grid lines
  — Measurement of the space between grid lines

❏ Table
  — Meaning of values for the Active property
  — Meaning of values for the Size property
  — Meaning of values for the Visible property

As you can see, some ideas are repeated: the usefulness of a grid and some property information. However, the passage does not deal clearly with what it means for the grid to be visible and what it means for the grid to be active.

Revision

You can display a grid (a set of horizontal and vertical lines) on forms to help you place components. You can control these aspects of the grid:

❏ Whether objects automatically align with the grid
❏ Size of the vertical and horizontal space between grid lines
❏ Whether the grid is visible

You will probably want the grid to be visible and active, so that you can use it as you create objects or move them. However, objects will also align with the grid when it is invisible and active.

Table 1 gives the possible values for the Active, Size, and Visible properties of a grid.

Table 1. Properties of a grid and how to use them

Property	Possible Values	Default	Use to ...
Active	True False	True	Make an object align with the grid lines Place an object anywhere on the form
Size	45 to 1485 twips*	5 pixels	Set vertical space between lines with Size.Width=Int Set horizontal space between lines with Size.Height=Int
Visible	True False	True	Make the grid visible Make the grid invisible

* A twip is a unit of measure that represents one-twentieth of a point. The term derives from TWentieth of an Inch Point. There are 72 points in an inch, 1440 twips in an inch, and 567 twips in a centimeter. Use twips as a measurement independent of screen resolution.

The flow of ideas in the revision is:

- ❏ Paragraph 1
  - — Usefulness of a grid (including definition)
  - — List of the meaning of the properties

- ❏ Paragraph 2
  - — Relationship of visible and active
  - — Relationship of invisible and active

- ❏ Paragraph 3
  - — Introduction to the table

- ❏ Table
  - — How to make grid lines active
  - — How to change the space between grid lines
  - — How to make grid lines visible

The revision flows and includes needed information without being redundant. It includes the definition of a grid but emphasizes the value of a grid to the user. Online information could link to a definition rather than include it here. The revision also includes a definition of twip but as a note to the table rather than as text.

The revision relates the text to the table by using a list to emphasize the meaning of the properties. The list treats all three properties, and then a paragraph goes into more detail about the relationship between the Visible and Active properties. This detail is warranted because the relationship is not obvious.

Writers sometimes use transitions less in reference information, which users tend to sample rather than read consecutively, or in online information, where space is at a premium. In these situations, headings are a clear way to change a subject or to express the purpose of a chunk of information.

Present similar topics in a similar way

One way to help users understand information the first time is to present similar topics in a similar way. This guideline applies to both the content and the format of technical information. It therefore overlaps completeness ("Use patterns of information to ensure proper coverage" on page 62), organization ("Organize information consistently" on page 146), style ("Follow style guidelines" on page 129), and visual effectiveness ("Use visual elements logically and consistently" on page 216).

Here are some ways to present similar information:

- ❏ Use the same notation for the syntax of a programming language in all online and printed information.
- ❏ If you enclose some figures in boxes, enclose all the figures.
- ❏ If you describe one of the four benefits of a product in terms of a problem the product solves, describe the other three benefits that way.
- ❏ If you explain some procedures through annotated examples, explain them all that way.

You might accomplish the first two items by following style guidelines or using graphical elements consistently. The last two items require more attention to the content. You need to decide whether clarity is best served by such consistent treatment of the topic.

Use lists appropriately

Suit the type of list to the information. Use an ordered list for information where the sequence or priority is important. Instructions in procedures are the most common use of ordered lists in technical information. Use an unordered list for items of similar importance, such as a set of alternatives or parts. Both kinds of lists are used appropriately in the following passage.

Passage with both kinds of lists

Entering the Shortcut text

You can add the encoded shortcut text in either of two ways:

❑ Add the text in the item's selected text in the Menu Editor outline.
❑ Edit the ShortCut property of the selected item using the Property Editor.

To enter a shortcut for the Copy command:

1. In the Menu Editor window, double-click the Copy item.

   The Property Editor opens, displaying the properties of Copy.

2. Set the ShortCut property to the ^{ins}.

3.

Keep list items parallel, to avoid the confusion in the following passage.

Original

Help

If the new file has the same name as an existing file,
do one of the following:

❑ Specify the REPLACE option, to replace the existing file.
❑ Give the file a new name (RENAMEoption).
❑ By indicating IGNORE, stop processing the file.

Revision

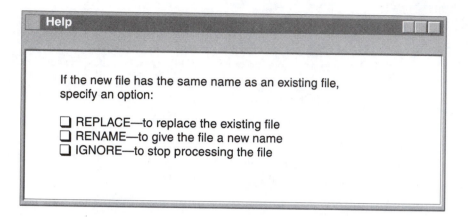

> **Help**
>
> If the new file has the same name as an existing file,
> specify an option:
>
> ☐ REPLACE—to replace the existing file
> ☐ RENAME—to give the file a new name
> ☐ IGNORE—to stop processing the file

At first glance, the two passages look alike: each is a list with three items. However, in the original passage, each item focuses on an action only superficially; users puzzle over unexpected turns. In the revision, the items focus on the options and are consistent; users can predict what's coming. The items in the list have a similar structure. This similar structure is called *parallelism*.

Segment information into tables

Like lists, tables can effectively present similar technical information in a similar way.

Spread information across the columns. Some tables lump too much information in one column, often the last column, as in the following table.

Original

Option	Default	Comments
CalStackSize	10	CalStackSize=15 Sets the number of displayable items in the combination box for the Inspector Call Stack
CreationMode	ControlArray	CreationMode=AskUser—User confirmation CreationMode=ControlArray—No warning CreationMode=IndividualControl—Group created from Toolbox
UndoStackSize	10	UndoStackSize=# For example, a value of 5 limits **Edit->Undo** and **Edit->Redo** to five actions each

Revision

Option	Default	Example	Explanation
CalStackSize	10	CalStackSize=15	Sets the number of displayable items in the combination box for the Inspector Call Stack
CreationMode	Control Array	CreationMode=AskUser CreationMode=ControlArray CreationMode=IndividualControl	Asks for user confirmation No warning needed Group created from Toolbox
UndoStackSize	10	UndoStackSize=5	Limits **Edit->Undo** and **Edit->Redo** to five actions each

The last column of the original table is a catchall for different kinds of information. The revision separates out a column for examples and a column for an explanation of the example.

Avoid using tables when the information you want to present is undifferentiated. Separate out the common information and put it in text rather than have a column with the same entries, as in the following passage.

Original

Data Type	Passed by Reference	Passed by Value
Integer	x	x
Long	x	x
Single	x	x
Double	x	x
Currency	x	x
String	x	x
Array	x	
Null pointers	x	
User defined	x	x
Variant	x	x
Any	x	
Class	x	

Revision

> All data types can be passed by reference. All data types except the following can be passed by value: array, null pointers, any, and class.

Unless you have more information to add to this table or you have no other reason to list the data types in one place, the information in this table might better be expressed in text, as in the revised passage.

Use technical terms only if they are necessary and appropriate

Whenever you can reasonably avoid a term that is peculiar to your product, do so. Unless a new term really helps users, it is just one more thing for them to learn.

Decide whether to use a term

When deciding whether a term is necessary and appropriate, consider these factors:

❏ Is there already a suitable term for the thing you want to name?

If there is a widely used and accepted term, use it. There's no need to coin a new term, even if you're tempted to replace a technical term with a nontechnical term.

❏ Do you intend to use a term only once or twice? If so, you might be able to use a descriptive phrase instead.

Do not create an acronym unless you will use it often, and then only if the phrase it stands for is unwieldy.

Are all the terms necessary in the following passage?

Original

> Each keyword describes one aspect of a program failure. A set of keywords, called a *keyword string*, describes a specific problem in detail. Because you use a keyword string to search a database, a keyword string is also called a *search argument*.

Revision

> Each keyword describes one aspect of a program failure. You use a set of keywords, called a *keyword string*, to describe a problem in detail, search a database for a similar problem, and obtain a fix for the problem.

The original passage introduces a term, *search argument*, that the user can probably get along without. The revised example uses generic words and focuses on the uses of the keywords rather than on adding to the user's vocabulary. Depending on the experience of the audience, you might also drop *keyword string* as unnecessary.

Clarity

Use terms consistently

If you decide that a term is needed, carefully choose it, introduce it, and use it:

❑ If the general literature in your field uses two or more terms for the same thing, pick one and use it consistently.

In some writing, you are encouraged to use different words for the same thing, for variety. In technical writing, however, more than one term for the same thing causes confusion. Two terms suggest two different things. For example, if people usually call something a *class*, don't call it a *type*. Users don't need a second term.

You might decide that using alternative terms with which users are familiar will help them understand a new concept. In that case, be sure to clearly identify the one term that you intend to use thereafter.

For example, you might deal with the similarity between *containment* and *aggregation* by writing "Containment (also known as *aggregation*) refers to the relationship in which a class is part of another class."

❑ Consider whether the term suggests what it means.

If it suggests nothing, users must learn it by rote. If it suggests something that is different from what it means, users will be confused.

❑ Carefully choose terms that indicate distinctions among things.

For example, a better contrasting term for *physical records* might have been *nonphysical records* rather than *logical records*, which suggests *illogical records* as its opposite. Physical records and logical records are common terms today and should not be changed. However, new users of these terms might understand them more easily if the distinction between them were more apparent in the words.

❑ Be sensitive to whether a term is jargon.

Jargon is a kind of shortcut that people on your project use or maybe that is used throughout your company or by a small group of professionals. Such a term might play off another word, as *automagically* plays off *automatically*. It might have a different meaning from what's generally expected, as in *hit* or *check* used to refer to an error in software or hardware, or *platform* to refer to an operating system. It might be a truncation or elongation of the regular term.

Avoid using such a term unless it is appropriate for your audience and there is no other word that fits the situation.

Developing Quality Technical Information

Define each term that is new to the intended audience

In all writing, the transactions between the writer and the user of the information depend on the vocabulary they have in common.

When users first encounter a new subject, it might seem like a foreign language, with its own vocabulary and rules for combining the concepts that the terms express. Native speakers of English who have never developed a computer application might feel as lost as if they were in a foreign country the first time they try to use an application development tool.

Some terms might be familiar, but their definitions might differ from what users expect. *Object* and *class,* for example, are familiar words, but they have special meanings in object-oriented programming.

You must define terms that are new to users or are used differently from what users expect. Such terms include acronyms and other abbreviations.

Explain a new term in text where you first use the term in a meaningful way and highlight the term. Try not to use the term in passing before that, but sometimes such usage cannot be avoided.

To help users recognize the terms and definitions you use, highlight new terms. In online information, make the definition available through a link. You can also have links from acronyms to the terms that they stand for. However, it's probably easier on users if you use an acronym in online information only after you give the term in the same help window or if the acronym is commonly understood; you can't be sure that the user has seen another help window that explains the acronym.

In printed information, include a definition where you first use a new term and put the term in a glossary. If a term has an acronym or abbreviation that you use, spell out the first occurrence of the term, and follow it with the acronym or abbreviation in parentheses.

Including an example in the definition also helps users understand terms.

Original

| attribute | An intrinsic characteristic of a class or object: it can have a value. |

Revision

| attribute | An intrinsic characteristic of a class or object: it can have a value. For example the attributes of a driver for a car insurance application might include birth date, gender and traffic violations. Values for these attributes might be 05/03/19 78, female, and 0. |

The original definition is abstract and hard to understand. The revised definition makes more sense because it draws on common experience to clarify the meaning of *attribute*.

In definitions, use terms that are familiar to the user, or define those terms also. If you use terms that you must also define, be careful that the definitions aren't circular. Try to make the definitions independent of each other.

Original

index entry	A <u>key</u> and a <u>pointer</u> paired together
key	One half of the pair that makes up an index entry.
pointer	One half of the pair that makes up an index entry.

Revision

index entry	A <u>key</u> and a <u>pointer</u> paired together.
key	One or more consecutive characters taken from a data record; used to identify the record and establish its sequence.
pointer	An address or other indication of location.

The original definitions of *key* and *pointer* merely paraphrase the definition of *index entry*. The revised definitions are informative.

Make sure that new terms are compatible with each other and with existing terms. If you define two terms separately, define the combination only if it has a special significance. For example, you wouldn't need to define *class attribute* if you've defined *class* and *attribute*. However, you'd probably define *data type* rather than *data* and *type* because of their widespread use together.

In sum

Use the guidelines in this chapter to ensure that technical information is clear to your audience. Refer to the examples in the chapter for practical applications of these guidelines.

When you review technical information for clarity, you can use this checklist in two ways:

- ❑ As a reminder of what to look for, to ensure a thorough review
- ❑ As an evaluation tool, to determine the quality of the information

You can apply the quality rating in the third column of the checklist to the guideline as a whole. Judging by the number and severity of items you found, decide how the information rates on each guideline for this quality characteristic. You can then add your findings to "Quality Checklist" on page 269, which covers all the quality characteristics.

Although the guidelines are intended to cover all areas for this quality characteristic, you might find additional items to add to the list for a guideline.

 Clarity

Guidelines for clarity	Items to look for	Quality rating
Focus on the meaning.	• Sentences are not unnecessarily long. • Paragraphs do not ramble. • Verbs are precise. • Meaningless words are not used. • Only necessary modifiers are used.	1 2 3 4 5
Avoid ambiguity	• Words are easy to translate. • Antecedents of pronouns are immediately apparent. • Modifiers are placed appropriately. • There are no long strings of nouns. • Expressions are positive.	1 2 3 4 5
Keep elements short.	• Expressions are concise. • Words are direct. • The length of lists is appropriate for the content and medium.	1 2 3 4 5
Write cohesively.	• Transitions are smooth. • Lists, tables, and examples are integrated.	1 2 3 4 5
Present similar information in a similar way.	• Types of lists are appropriate for the information. • List items are parallel in structure. • Tables are well segmented.	1 2 3 4 5
Use technical terms only if they are necessary and appropriate.	• Terms used are needed. • Terms are appropriate. • Use of terms is consistent. • Jargon is not used.	1 2 3 4 5
Define each term that is new to the intended audience.	• Terms are defined. • Acronyms and abbreviations are defined. • Definitions are easy to understand.	1 2 3 4 5

Note: The scale for the quality rating goes from very satisfied (1) to very dissatisfied (5).

Developing Quality Technical Information

Chapter 6

Concreteness

Concreteness in technical information communicates what people can see, hear, smell, taste, or touch—not just what they can think. It deals with material things and physical actions in the real world.

Technical subjects such as relational database access, inheritance among classes, and communication protocols are abstract: users cannot experience them directly. Few users enjoy wandering among concepts and grasping at new terms without being able to connect them to something real in their experience.

Language and presentations can run the gamut from the abstract (or general) to the concrete (or specific):

Abstract			Concrete
financial institution	bank	Federated Bank	Federated Bank, San Jose
computer system	software	database	Lotus Notes
hierarchy	pyramid structure	organization chart	organization chart, ABC Company
"A function of the compiler is to check syntax."		"The COBOL compiler checks syntax."	example of syntax messages for a code sample
"A database is a set of tables, in which each table is a set of relations."			"A database is like a file drawer, in which each folder holds related papers."

Because people can more easily understand the concrete, a good technical writer relates the abstract to the concrete.

Because ot the importance of examples and scenarios to users, this chapter focuses on them and on the characteristics that make examples effective, such as accuracy and retrievability.

To make information concrete, follow these guidelines:

- ❏ **Choose examples that are appropriate for the audience and topic.**
- ❏ **Use realistic, accurate, up-to-date examples.**
- ❏ **Make examples easy to find.**
- ❏ **Use scenarios to illustrate tasks and provide overviews.**
- ❏ **Use code examples that users can easily adapt.**
- ❏ **Relate unfamiliar information to familiar information.**

Choose examples that are appropriate for the audience and topic

An *example* is a representative of a set of things.

Examples are probably the purest form of concreteness—and the most useful form of information for users. No matter how many you supply, users will probably ask for more.

Examples in technical information can go wrong in many ways. Usually the problem is that an example is too difficult, too easy, or in an inappropriate subject.

Original

> You can do many tasks from the InfoShopper main window. You can click Color to change the color of any of the windows. For example, click the red push button to make the window red.

Revision

> You can do many tasks from the InfoShopper main window. You can list the available merchandise in a category by clicking on the picture that corresponds to your category. For example, to see a list of jewelry, click the picture of a ring.

The original passage tries to show how easy the product is to use by presenting the ease of changing the color on the window. However, this example isn't pertinent to the user's main tasks.

The revised passage uses the task of listing merchandise to show how easy the product is to use. This task is something that users can relate to. Not only do the users learn how easy the product is to use, but also they learn how to perform a relevant task. Few elements help users learn faster to apply information than an example.

Users should be able to understand an example and apply it to their circumstances. You might need to have examples for different skill levels and from various subjects. As with so many guidelines, the key principle is to *know your user*. To understand the skill levels and get ideas for examples, check with your users, and check journals and documentation for similar products or for similar uses of different products.

You might wonder whether you should try to unify your examples around a particular situation. You might, for example, try to base them on various applications used by a fictional hotel or marketing firm. Some users prefer a variety of examples to unified examples that build on each other throughout the information. The main problem with unified examples is that they require users to be familiar with previous examples in the set.

Consider also the need to appeal to an international audience. Avoid situations and terms that are specific to a particular culture, as in the following example:

Original

Valid Names	Not Valid Names	Rule
inch	3inch	Name must start with letter or underscore.
retirement_account OS2	computer invoice OS/2	Name must not use special characters (other than underscore) or blanks.

Revision

Valid Names	Not Valid Names	Rule
centimeter	3centimeter	Name must start with letter or underscore.
savings_account OS2	computer invoice OS/2	Name must not use special characters (other than underscore) or blanks.

The original list of examples uses terms such as *inch* and *retirement account* that might not be common outside the United States. The revised list replaces these terms with ones that are more likely to be international.

110

Examples of commands provide valuable information to users about syntax and usage. The following passage requires the user to read the explanation of the syntax carefully and provides no example for the user to follow.

Original

> To continue a line without adding a blank space, follow the last character on the first line with a quotation mark, a blank space, a concatenation operator, and a comma.

Revision

> To continue a command onto a second line, add the following string to the end of the first line:
>
> ` ' ||,`
>
> For example:
>
> ```
> 'TEST-STRING ,,,"Are you absol' ||,
> utely sure you want to exit?", ROW,COL'
> ```
>
> yields this result:
>
> ```
> 'TEST-STRING ,,,"Are you absolutely sure you want to exit?",ROW COL'
> ```

The revised passage shows users what they need to type to complete their task. It also provides both an example of the syntax and the equivalent result, in case the users are unfamiliar with the command in the example.

You might also provide samples such as:

❑ Sample databases so that users can practice populating databases with your product

❑ Sample applications that your users can use to practice testing an interface with your product

Original

> Before you use InfoBase, read the manual. It is important that you understand all the tasks before you use InfoBase with your database.
> -
> -
> -
>
> Sample SQL is provided in Appendix A. You can copy the samples from the appendix if you want to use them. For more information on how to write SQL statements, see the *SQL Operator's Guide*.

Revision

> You can practice performing the tasks in this chapter before you try them on your own database. Use the sample database provided with InfoBase instead of your own database until you are comfortable with the tasks. To access the sample database:
> -
> -
> -
>
> You can use the SQL that is provided in the SAMPLES directory for steps 3, 4, and 5. Or you can write your own SQL.

The original passage provides little help to users. It might actually frustrate them by setting such a high first hurdle as reading the whole manual, or scare them by implying serious consequences from trying to learn by trial and error. The revised passage indicates a friendly, task-oriented product that provides users with helpful samples they can use to perform their tasks.

Use realistic, accurate, up-to-date examples

To make a point and not spend a long time doing it, writers sometimes simplify examples. Writers seldom have real examples, espcially code examples, and permission to use them. Realistic (rather than real) examples are one possibility for filling the need for examples.

Regardless of whether an example is real or realistic, the parts that users depend on must be accurate. Inaccurate code examples can be worse than no code examples. Be sure to test code examples, although this testing requires extra effort. Code fragments and stand-alone examples probably need scaffolding (code that simulates the function of nonexistent components) to enable testers to test them. Sometimes reading such examples is the most that testers can fit in the testing schedule. Taking lines of code from a larger application is much easier, because you can assume that the parts are correct if the whole application works.

Original

> This statement gets the value of the attribute price, figures 5% of its current value, and stores the result in the variable $commission:
>
> ```
> getMult('price', 0.50, $commission)
> ```

Revision

> This statement gets the value of the attribute price, figures 5% of its current value, and stores the result in the variable $commission:
>
> ```
> getMult('price', 0.05, $commission)
> ```

The original example missed 5% by a factor of 10. A user would probably decide that the text was more likely to be right than the actual code. A tester reading the code example would probably also find this error, which the revised example corrects.

A code example can become outdated (and inaccurate) if it contains functions that are no longer supported. Code examples and other kinds of examples can become outdated if items from popular culture or numbers (such as prices and years) are involved. If you must include years, try to make them far enough in the future that they won't soon seem passe. Consider how long the information must last.

To reduce the work needed to maintain examples, remove items that are likely to show their age quickly.

Original

> This statement creates an object, an instance of the class car. Unless there is a later name, the product will use the name myBronco for the object and assign the name actually used to the variable mycar:
>
> ```
> car.new('myBronco', mycar)
> ```

Revision

> This statement creates an object, an instance of the class car. Unless there is a later name, the product will use the name myFord for the object and assign the name actually used to the variable mycar:
>
> ```
> car.new('myFord', mycar)
> ```

The original example uses a model name, which is more likely to change than the manufacturer name, which the revised example uses.

Whatever examples you use, be sure to make the explanatory text match the example.

Make examples easy to find

Examples can't help users much if they're hard to find. Rather than burying text examples in a paragraph, set them off, perhaps by starting a new paragraph, adding a heading, adding a column to a table, or using a list.

Original

> The InfoProduct maintains information about attributes that are unique to the image data type, as well as information about attributes that are common across data types (for example, common across the image and audio data types). For example, the product maintains information about the width, height, and format of an image, as well as information about common attributes such as the identification of the person who imported the object into the database or who last updated the object.

Revision

> The product maintains information about two kinds of attributes:
>
> ❏ Attributes that are unique to the image data type, such as the width, height, and format of an image
>
> ❏ Attributes that are common across data types, such as the identification of the person who last updated the object (whether an image, audio clip, or some other type of object)

The first passage repeats too much information for the sake of a few examples. The repeated information overwhelms the examples and makes them hard to find and understand. The revision uses a list to avoid repeating information and make the examples stand out.

Usability research shows that users prefer information that is closest to the product interface—even a click and scroll or function key away can be too much. The information needs to be part of the words and choices in the product interface. You can assimilate some information into the interface as examples, as in these cases:

❏ Where you might use contextual help for an entry field, use instead an example that shows both the default and the format.

❏ Use combination boxes to show users their choices for constructing a programming statement.

Look for places where you can replace text with examples rather than just add examples.

115

Use scenarios to illustrate tasks and provide product overviews

A *scenario* depicts a series of events over time, usually around a fictitious but realistic set of circumstances. It shows one path through the product, a path that can be broad or narrow, high or low, vertical or horizontal. It can range from a high-level overview to a sequence of interface manipulations (sometimes accompanied by captured windows).

You use scenarios primarily either to teach (as in a tutorial) or to describe and motivate (as in marketing information). Unlike lists of steps (as in a procedure), scenarios usually have a story that helps guide the actions. Consider the following introduction to a tutorial lesson:

Original

In this lesson you learn how to process data for more than one application server.

There are three ways to manage the transfer of the data:

- ☐ Use virtual memory as a buffer for holding a few rows of data.
- ☐ Use disk space as a buffer for holding many rows of data.
- ☐ Use multiprocessing to run each update in a different thread.

Revision

In this lesson you learn how to write an application to process data for more than one application server.

Suppose the DoItRight Corporation periodically sends a copy of the employee table that is stored at headquarters to the regional branches. The application you are writing needs to refresh the local copies. However, because a database manager can be connected to only one application server at a time, the application must manage the transfer of the data.

There are three ways to manage the transfer of the data:

- ☐ Use virtual memory as a buffer for holding a few rows of data.
- ☐ Use disk space as a buffer for holding many rows of data.
- ☐ Use multiprocessing to run each update in a different thread.

The original passage gives only the tasks, without a context in which to understand them. The revised passage puts the person in a realistic situation with a need to use the task information.

Consider the following sample passage from marketing information:

Original

> With a distributed relational database, you can reap the benefits of being able to access data as if it were located wherever you are.

Revision

> With a distributed relational database, you can reap the benefits of being able to access data as if it were located wherever you are.
>
> Consider a company with headquarters in one city and sales offices in many other cities. Each sales office has a relational database for its own transactions, and each month the office sends data to headquarters for the sales summary report. Using a distributed relational database that is a collection of the sales office databases, headquarters could access the sales data directly.

The original passage leaves it to the user's imagination what the benefits might be. The revised passage gives a scenario of a particular benefit that users can apply to similar situations.

Some writers make the mistake of thinking they've made a scenario just by adding a thin story layer to what is still hard-to-understand information, as in the following passage:

Original

> **Connection ID Usage**
>
> In this scenario, a two-party call exists between party A and party B. The Make_Call from party A to party B results in connection IDs being generated to represent their participation in the call. Party A then issues an Extend_Call program call to extend the call to party C. The Extend_Call places party B on hold and results in two new connection IDs being created: one for party A's connection in the new call and one for party C. To join all three parties in a conference call, party A issues a call to InfoConf specifying requesting party ID 1 and requesting party ID 2.

Revision

Conference Call and Connection IDs

Alice needs to set up a conference call with Bill and Calvin so that all three of them can have a discussion. Alice calls Bill, puts him on hold while she calls Calvin, and then connects Calvin into the call.

The implementation of this conference call in terms of connection IDs looks like this:

Event	Connection IDs
A calls B	a1, b1
A extends the call to C	a2, c1

The original scenario might represent a real situation inside the telephone software, but that's not where most people live or interact. Users might need to read this narrative several times just to understand whether the parties in it are people and what they are doing.

The revised scenario clarifies the situation and the connection between what the people do and what the software does in response.

When you use scenarios, focus on tasks that users are likely to want to perform. Scenarios that include interesting and relevant tasks are more helpful than those that focus on rarely used features.

Use code examples that users can easily adapt

Code examples help users do their own work because they can copy the example and adapt it to their needs.

Examples in software information often contain code and commands. A C++ routine does not describe C++ code; it *is* C++ code for a particular purpose. When describing the C++ language, a good writer uses examples of C++ code.

Some code examples are hard to understand and use because they use ambiguous variables or lack explanatory comments.

Original

```
/* */
parse arg s n'('p
if s = '' then s = 's'
if n = '' then n = '<n>'
if p = '' then p = '<p>'
'extract /line'
'bot'
'i 's'--'strip(n)', 'p
':'line.1
'no' substr(date(month),1,3)
```

Revision

```
/* Add a salutation to a note and change the notebook */
parse arg salutation name '('phoneNumber
if salutation = '' then salutation = 'thanks'
if name = '' then name = '<your name>'
if phoneNumber = '' then phoneNumber = '<and number>'
'extract /line'
'bottom'
'input 'salutation'--'strip(name)', 'phoneNumber
':'line.1
/* Call the no macro to change the notebook to the current month */
'no' substr(date(month),1,3)
```

The original code example is hard to understand because it has no comments and uses variables that are too short to suggest what they represent. The revision remedies these problems.

119

When you add comments to code examples, consider where they will be most helpful—probably not far from what they're explaining.

Original

> The following example creates a user-defined function (UDF) named map_scale that calculates the scale of a map. Notice that the UDF identifies map as the data type to which it can be applied. The code that implements the function is written in C and is identified in the EXTERNAL NAME clause.
>
> ```
> /* */
> CREATE FUNCTION map_scale (map)
>    RETURNS SMALLINT 's'
>    EXTERNAL NAME 'scale!map'
>    LANGUAGE C
>    PARAMETER STYLE DB2SQL
>    NO SQL
>    NOT VARIANT
>    NO EXTERNAL ACTION
> ```

Revision

> The following example creates a user-defined function (UDF) named map_scale that calculates the scale of a map.
>
> ```
> /* map is the data type to which map_scale applies */
> CREATE FUNCTION map_scale (map)
>    RETURNS SMALLINT 's'
> /* scale!map is the name of the C function that implements the UDF */
>    EXTERNAL NAME 'scale!map'
>    LANGUAGE C
>    PARAMETER STYLE DB2SQL
>    NO SQL
>    NOT VARIANT
>    NO EXTERNAL ACTION
> ```

The original passage uses sentences outside the code to give information that is more clearly presented in the revised passage as comments in the code. Users can easily miss the information when it is separate from the code. Also, the comments are there for users to see if they access the code online.

If your examples are large sections of code, provide them online with the product, rather than only in printed information. Users need to transcribe large code examples that are not online before they can copy or adapt the code.

Relate unfamiliar information to familiar information

Comparing the unfamiliar with the familiar makes users feel more comfortable with new information.

Similes and analogies are the explicit description of one thing in terms of another. They add color and interest as well. It is difficult for some users, for example, to understand what a database is. But when they read that tables in a database are like folders in a file drawer, they can understand because they have used folders and file drawers.

However, similes and analogies can introduce unwanted associations and emotions. Therefore, when you use similes and analogies, make the basis of comparison explicit. Avoid using metaphors, which are implied descriptions of one thing in terms of another.

Original

> A *class hierarchy* is a ranking of classes that shows their inheritance relationships. It looks like a tree.

Revision

> A *class hierarchy* is a ranking of classes that shows their inheritance relationships. It resembles the roots of a tree in that the classes lower in the structure are connected to classes higher up.

The original passage makes a vague assertion about the likeness of a class hierarchy to a tree. Various pictures of trees are likely to come to mind, but you don't know why they might look like a class hierarchy. The revised passage gives a reason for the suggested likeness.

121

Original

> **Help** ▢▢▢
>
> You can use the InfoSupport shared folders function
> to store and retrieve information on the system.
> It increases the amount of information you can use.

Revision

> **Help** ▢▢▢
>
> Like a library, your computer stores a great deal of
> information. In a library, not all the information is
> necessarily within easy reach. For example, in some
> libraries you might need to use a ladder to reach books
> stored on the top shelves.
>
> Your computer also provides a ladder to retrieve
> information. You can use the InfoSupport shared folders
> function as your ladder to store and retrieve information on
> the system. It increases the amount of information
> you can use.

The original passage states the facts but lacks immediacy. The revised passage uses an analogy that many people can visualize and understand.

Often technical information deals with subjects that are new to at least some users. If subject matter is well understood by most people, there is no gap to bridge and no need to use similes or analogies.

In sum

Use the guidelines in this chapter to ensure that technical information is concrete rather than abstract. Refer to the examples in the chapter for practical applications of these guidelines.

When you review technical information for concreteness, you can use this checklist in two ways:

❏ As a reminder of what to look for, to ensure a thorough review
❏ As an evaluation tool, to determine the quality of the information

You can apply the quality rating in the third column of the checklist to the guideline as a whole. Judging by the number and severity of items you found, decide how the information rates on each guideline for this quality characteristic. You can then add your findings to "Quality Checklist" on page 269, which covers all the quality characteristics.

Although the guidelines are intended to cover all areas for this quality characteristic, you might find additional items to add to the list for a guideline.

Guidelines for concreteness	Items to look for	Quality rating
Choose examples that are appropriate for the audience and topic.	• There are enough examples and scenarios. • Syntax explanations contain examples. • Examples and scenarios are appropriate. • Text that is introduced as an example is an example. • Samples are provided.	1 2 3 4 5
Use realistic, accurate, up-to-date examples.	• Examples are realistic. • Code examples are accurate and up to date. • Textual examples are accurate and up to date. • Scenarios are up to date.	1 2 3 4 5
Make examples easy to find.	• Textual examples are easy to find. • Code examples are easy to find.	1 2 3 4 5
Use scenarios to illustrate tasks and provide product overviews.	• Scenarios are provided where needed. • Scenarios are not abstract.	1 2 3 4 5
Use code examples that users can easily adapt.	• Code examples are clear. • Code examples have comments. • Large code examples are provided online.	1 2 3 4 5
Relate unfamiliar information to familiar information.	• Analogies and similes are provided where needed. • Analogies and similes are focused.	1 2 3 4 5

Note: The scale for the quality rating goes from very satisfied (1) to very dissatisfied (5).

Chapter 7

Style

Style is the correctness and appropriateness of writing conventions and choices of words and phrases. Developing a style for technical information means following certain conventions or rules to ensure consistency, as well as making choices about tone and presentation. Style is an expression of the "look and feel" of information.

Usually, a particular industry has a style manual of choice. The newspaper industry has the *AP Stylebook* and the *UPI Stylebook*. The medical industry follows the *American Medical Association* guidelines. Academic and technical publishing houses generally follow *The Chicago Manual of Style*.

Many companies that publish technical information have style guidelines that cover conventions in finer detail than a manual like the *Chicago Manual*. There are also situations that the *Chicago Manual* doesn't deal with, such as online information and reference material that isn't read sequentially. At a lower level, a specific project might have its own detailed guidelines that cover situations in which the project style differs from other guidelines.

In addition to using written guidelines, writers must often decide what *tone* to use. The choice and arrangement of words in a sentence affect the tone of a piece of writing. For example, if you're writing a marketing brochure, you probably want to use a different tone than for a reference manual.

As a writer or reviewer of information, you need to be aware of the latest style conventions that apply to your project. You also need to understand the target audience, so that you can determine the appropriate tone to use.

To make information stylistically correct and appropriate, follow these guidelines:

❏ **Use correct grammar, spelling, and punctuation.**

❏ **Follow style guidelines.**

❏ **Use an active style.**

❏ **Use the imperative mood for instructions.**

❏ **Use appropriate and consistent tone.**

Use correct grammar, spelling, and punctuation

Many of us assume that the grammar, spelling, and punctuation that we use is correct—after all, it's what we learned in school. But often there are ambiguities in spelling and punctuation, and grammar can be colloquial or distracting.

For example, UK English spells some words differently than American English, such as colour and color, catalogue and catalog. Some industries, such as the newspaper industry, prefer not to use a serial comma before a conjunction, whereas in technical writing it is often necessary.

Grammatical errors are sometimes easy to make but hard to detect, because the rules for speaking are less strict than for writing. This is especially true for writing that is intended for a worldwide audience. Some problems to avoid in technical writing are misplaced modifiers, noun-pronoun disagreement, and dangling participles.

The following passage shows how restrictive and nonrestrictive clauses can be a problem.

Original

> The tool kit provides a set of utilities which exploits some of the new features of InfoBase Version 2.

Revision

> The tool kit provides a set of utilities that exploits some of the new features of InfoBase Version 2.

The original passage uses the word *which* ambiguously. A translator might interpret the *which* clause as nonrestrictive even though the clause is not preceded by a comma. The sentence might be interpreted as meaning that the tool kit provides only one set of utilities, when in fact the passage refers to a specific set of utilities out of many sets.

The revised passage shows a simple, but important, correction: using *that* to indicate that the modifying clause is meant to be restrictive.

Style

The following passage shows several style problems. Can you find them all?

Original

> For mailings, you could use the new InfoProduct Executive Summary, a two sided colour factsheet which:
>
> ❏ Describes the product
> ❏ Shows some screen captures
> ❏ Lists the hardware and software required

Revision

> For mailings, you can use the new InfoProduct Executive Summary, a two-sided color fact sheet that provides:
>
> ❏ Product description
> ❏ Screen captures
> ❏ Hardware and software requirements

In the first passage, ambiguous use of *which*, a missing hyphen, colloquial spelling, and improperly compounded words are all style problems. In addition, the word *could* is weak and ambivalent, and the verbs in the list items aren't necessary. The revised passage corrects all these problems.

Follow style guidelines

Much of what we consider style evolves from the experience of editors, writers, and designers. Particular writing projects must apply certain conventions to new information. Usually, these conventions are determined before you start writing, and are documented as guidelines.

For the user's convenience, the uniform presentation of information is important. Guidelines help ensure that different writers working on related information do not introduce variations that can confuse users.

Sometimes writers might not have a set of established guidelines, and need to decide what conventions to use. If you find yourself in this situation, consider the following advice:

1. Consult relevant authoritative sources for similar situations. Check more than one source to see whether authorities disagree on the subject. For a list of some popular style manuals, see "Easy to Understand" on page 289.

2. If there are no obvious similar situations, isolate the underlying issue. Look for precedents that apply to the issue or for guidelines that define style conventions in the general area.

3. Consider the effect of carrying out possible style decisions. How easy would each be to apply, probably by people other than just yourself? Is the reasoning straightforward, or does it have some exceptions?

4. Consider the effect on the user. Is the user likely to benefit from this style decision? Be confused by it? Need to stop and wonder why?

Whatever your source for style guidelines, if you follow it consistently, you'll provide your users with a reliable presentation that won't interfere with their ability to use the information.

Here are a few style issues to consider for any technical information:

Provide practical and consistent highlighting

When highlighting is used consistently and predictably, the reader doesn't need to stop and think about why a certain term is in boldface and another in italics, or what the difference is between entering a command displayed in lowercase and one displayed in all capital letters.

Assume each of the instructions in the following example is from different parts of a product's online help.

Original

> Press "ENTER."
>
> .
> .
> .
>
> Enter the `Search` command.
>
> .
> .
> .
>
> At a command prompt, type: `help` and press *Enter.*

Revision

> Press Enter.
>
> .
> .
> .
>
> Enter the SEARCH command.
>
> .
> .
> .
>
> At a command prompt, type `help` and press Enter.

The problems are obvious when looking at the original instructions together. The word *enter* appears in three different styles, two of them applying to the same usage. The second and third instructions use the same highlighting for different situations. Different types of highlighting are used to refer to a key; even if an explanation of highlighting is given, these discrepancies cannot be easily reconciled.

The revised instructions reduce the amount of highlighting and do not use conflicting styles. A user who is quickly scanning instructions will not stumble over the confusing highlighting of the original style.

Present list items consistently

Rules for list items vary depending on whose guidelines you are using, but here are some good ones to follow:

❑ Start each list item with a capital letter.

❏ If one list item ends with a period, use periods on all items.

❏ If none of the list items is a full sentence, don't use periods on any.

❏ Clearly introduce all lists.

❏ Make all list items grammatically parallel.

How many of these problems can you find in the following passage?

Original

> Changing the screen colors also changes the colors used for the keys. See Chapter 27, "Utilities Configuration" for more information about setting screen colors.
>
> | | |
> |---|---|
> | **Black on cyan** | The key is not pressed. |
> | **White on black** | You have pressed the key, and it is working correctly. |
> | **Red on black** | Key was held down, auto-repeat function activated. |

The original passage discusses changing the screen colors, but does not include an appropriate lead-in to the list describing screen colors and keyboard actions. The cross-reference before the list further complicates the meaning of the list. In addition, the list definitions vary in structure.

Revision

> Changing the screen colors also changes the colors used for the keys. The following list shows the default color scheme for the keys:
>
> | | |
> |---|---|
> | **Black on cyan** | No key was pressed. |
> | **White on black** | The key was pressed and is working correctly. |
> | **Red on black** | The key is held down, activating the auto-repeat function. |
>
> See Chapter 27, "Utilities Configuration" for more information about setting screen colors.

The revised passage introduces the list appropriately and places the cross-reference at the end of the passage. Presenting the definitions in consistent form further improves the list.

Use gender-neutral language

Avoid using *he* and *she* in technical information. Instead, use plurals, the imperative mood, or second person to restructure the sentence, as in the following examples. Just be sure to use one method, rather than a mix of several.

Original

> If the programmer keeps an accurate account of his programming time, he can determine his productivity.

The original passage can be revised in several ways to eliminate the use of *he* and *his*:

Revision using plural

> If programmers keep an accurate account of their programming time, they can determine their productivity.

Revision using imperative

> Keep an accurate account of your programming time so that you can determine your productivity.

Revision using second person

> If you keep an accurate account of your programming time, you can determine your productivity.

Or you can write the passage as an example, using a person's name:

Revision using person's name

> For example, if Susan keeps an accurate account of her programming time, she can determine her productivity.

Depending on the context of a particular passage, you can use any one of the previous styles to avoid gender-specific pronouns. But be careful to avoid constructions that mix a singular noun with a plural pronoun:

If the programmer keeps an accurate account of their time...

Use an active style

Writing directly to the user is the best way to convey information. Passive voice often makes it difficult for the user to understand who is doing the acting. Complex verb tenses (for example: future, past, past perfect) and verbals (gerund, participle, and infinitive) further hinder communication. Use the active voice and present tense to engage the reader.

Consider the following sentence:

Original

> It is possible to type up to 256 characters in the entry field.

Revision

> You can type up to 256 characters in the entry field.

The message is clear in both the original and the revised passage, but the revised passage actively engages the user. Any time you see a phrase such as "it is possible," consider rewriting the sentence to be more direct.

There are times when passive voice is appropriate. If the receiver of the action is more important than the agent (usually in the description of a process), use passive voice for the proper emphasis.

Original

> The system saves the file to the database.

Revision

> The file is saved to the database.

The original passage indicates an action (*saves*), and an agent of the action (*the system*). However, the important part of the passage is the fact that the file gets saved; the system doesn't matter.

Style

Use the imperative mood for instructions

The imperative mood expresses a command or request. With its implied *you*, the imperative mood directly addresses the user and makes it clear what action the user should perform.

Original

> The application should be started.

First Revision

> You need to start the application.

Second Revision

> Start the application.

Assume that the passage in the example comes from a procedure. Clearly, the original passage is not telling the user to perform an action. The first revision is an improvement in that it brings the user into the picture, but still describes an action to perform, rather than telling the user to do it. The second revision shows the instruction as it should be: in the imperative mood.

If a step in a set of instructions must be in the imperative mood, then it follows also that the response of the system should not be treated as a step on its own. For example, "A confirmation window opens" can be part of a step but should not be a separate step.

Use appropriate and consistent tone

The tone of writing is how it "sounds," how it feels to the reader. An appropriate tone allows the user to perform the task, learn the concepts, or make the right decisions without having to interpret your rhetoric.

The tone of technical information must be helpful; writing concrete and accurate information establishes a helpful tone. The tone must be direct; writing clear information establishes a direct tone. The tone must also be authoritative; writing task-oriented, concrete, complete, and accurate information establishes an authoritative tone.

Many kinds of tone are possible in technical writing. To achieve the tone that works best in a particular situation, you must know your audience. For example, a popular line of computer books addresses end users who want the basics foremost, and details only at an easy-to-grasp level. The authors of this series of books write in a very friendly, even humorous tone. The information is fun to read, yet complete and accurate.

Some products have excellent online help with a tone that is spare and direct without being dry. Procedural steps are delivered in brief statements, and explanations focus on the best way to do something, rather than explaining every angle.

In the following passage, the writer is trying to be friendly in providing a requirement.

Original

> Of course, you may not be able to print in this mode if you don't first define your printer.

Revision

> You must define your printer before printing in this mode.

The original passage might be appropriate in a discussion between co-workers, but in not technical information, The revised passage eliminates the awkwardness of the original.

Another consideration for tone is whether the information can be translated easily. Much technical information is translated into many languages, each of which can reflect cultural differences. To help translators, use a straightforward, noncolloquial style. Avoid idioms, which nearly always cause problems with internationalization. In addition, be sure to write so that non-native speakers in English aren't alienated by the tone.

Original

> To assist any investigative bureau in tracking the status of activities...

Revision

> To help you track the status of activities . . .

The original passage, in an attempt at humor, refers to an agency that might not be perceived in a positive light in many areas of the world.

The revision places the emphasis on tracking the status of activities—the actual function being discussed—rather than on some entity that could be considered threatening.

When writing for the World Wide Web, use a tone that is engaging and friendly. A word of caution, however: people all over the world access the Web, so you need to write for an international audience. Your Web pages can be lively and entertaining, while maintaining a tone that is professional and considerate of non-native speakers of English.

Original

> InfoTool is bending over backwards to be accommodating.

Revision

> InfoTool now offers several options, giving you the flexibility you need.

Although "bending over backwards" is an idiom most native English speakers have heard and understand, it is difficult to picture it applied to a software tool!

The revised passage expresses the same message in a style that is descriptive without being baffling.

In sum

Use the guidelines in this chapter to ensure that technical information has the correct and appropriate style for your audience. Refer to the examples in the chapter for practical applications of these guidelines.

When you review technical information for correctness and appropriateness of style, you can use this checklist in two ways:

❑ As a reminder of what to look for, to ensure a thorough review
❑ As an evaluation tool, to determine the quality of the information

You can apply the quality rating in the third column of the checklist to the guideline as a whole. Judging by the number and severity of items you found, decide how the information rates on each guideline for this quality characteristic. You can then add your findings to "Quality Checklist" on page 269, which covers all the quality characteristics.

Although the guidelines are intended to cover all areas for this quality characteristic, you might find additional items to add to the list for a guideline.

Guidelines for style	Items to look for	Quality rating
Use correct grammar, spelling, and punctuation.	• There are no grammatical errors. • There are no grammatical inconsistencies. • There are no denigrated terms. • Terms are spelled correctly.	1 2 3 4 5
Follow style guidelines.	• List items are consistent. • Elements conform to the style guidelines. • Text highlighting is consistent and explained.	1 2 3 4 5
Use an active style.	• The agents of verbs are apparent. • Shifts in tense or voice are appropriate.	1 2 3 4 5
Use the imperative mood for instructions.	• Instructions are not buried in passive voice. • Response of the system is not treated as a step.	1 2 3 4 5
Use appropriate and consistent tone.	• The tone is appropriate for the intended audience. • The tone is consistent.	1 2 3 4 5

Note: The scale for the quality rating goes from very satisfied (1) to very dissatisfied (5).

Part 3

Easy to Find

Finding information is essential, whether you're a new user trying to figure out where to start and what to do or an experienced user looking for a parameter for a command. The organization, retrievability, and visual effectiveness of information contribute most to whether users can find the information they need.

Chapter 8

Organization

Organization is the arrangement of smaller elements to make up larger elements—how things fit together. Well-organized information is easy to find, especially when the organization is obvious to the user.

Good organization can accommodate change more easily. Poorly organized documents are often littered with notes, boxes, and footnotes to make places for information that doesn't fit the pattern. Organizing a document well might take more time, but doing so will better serve the user and you in the long run.

You need to determine what users want to know and then organize your documents to best present that information to them. Sound simple? Don't be too sure. Organization spans more than just "In what order do I put the chapters in this document?"

Online information, for example, can contain conceptual, task, and contextual help, in addition to tutorials, cue cards, and more. Tasks contain steps, and steps contain actions and results. Similarly, printed documentation can be organized into books, books into parts and chapters, and chapters into sections. Starting at the bottom of the structure, you can organize sentences into topics, and topics into the larger elements.

You also need effective transitions or links, introductions, and topic emphasis throughout the text. All of these elements must work together to make information well organized.

To make information well organized, follow these guidelines:

- ❑ **Organize guidance information sequentially.**
- ❑ **Organize reference information logically.**
- ❑ **Organize information consistently.**
- ❑ **Organize help into discrete topics and types.**
- ❑ **Emphasize main points, subordinate secondary points.**
- ❑ **Divide a topic only if it has at least two subtopics.**
- ❑ **Branch only when helpful to the user.**
- ❑ **Reveal how the pieces fit together.**

Organize guidance information sequentially

Users usually complete task steps in a certain order, and the information should be arranged in a similar order. For example, a task with five subtasks suggests five sections of information. If what users do in subtask Y depends on what they have done in X, subtask X should precede subtask Y.

The following outline shows an organization that doesn't correspond to the actual order of tasks.

Original

Getting Started
    Planning for Installation
    Verifying Prerequisite Software Is Installed
    Installing InfoProduct
    Configuring InfoProduct
    Verifying Installation
    Removing InfoProduct

Revision

Getting Started
    Planning for Installation
    Verifying Prerequisite Software Is Installed
    Installing InfoProduct
    Verifying Installation
    Configuring InfoProduct

The original outline shows that the task of verifying installation follows the configuring task. Common sense suggests users are best served if they verify their installation before they configure the product, as shown in the revised outline. In addition, the original outline lists the task of removing InfoProduct as a getting started task. Users are not likely to remove a product right after they configure it. The revised outline shows that the document does not include the removing task with the other getting started tasks.

Sometimes users need to understand the concepts behind a task before they perform the task. In these cases, the structure of the information should facilitate learning—for example, from known to unknown and from the general rule to instances.

143

The following passage shows a task in which the first step assumes the users understand how to use the interface.

Original

> To place an item on hold:
>
> 1. Select the item from the Merchandise window.
> 2.

Revision

> The Merchandise window contains all the available items in the catalog. The items are nested logically by department, type, brand, description, size, and color. To select an item, move through the tree in the Merchandise window by expanding the branches (for example, expand the Children's branch, then the Shoes branch, and so on) until you select the item you want.
>
> To place an item on hold:
>
> 1. Select the item from the Merchandise window.
> 2.

New users might not be able to perform step 1 in the original passage without additional help. The revised passage prefaces the task steps with a general explanation of how to use the window.

Online help writers could link the first step of the original passage to the additional information on how to select an item from the Merchandise window.

Organize reference information logically

With reference information, the user's primary task is to find a piece of information, for whatever reason. When you provide reference information, you don't presuppose a particular task. Your focus is on helping users find the information.

Arranging reference information alphabetically or numerically works for all users. For example, an alphabetical arrangement tells the user who's looking at the entry "List" to go forward to get to "Store" and backward to get to "Copy."

Other arrangement schemes (such as by component or category, by job responsibility, or chronological) might be helpful to experienced users.

The following reference section shows an alphabetical organization.

Original

Reference Information
  ABC Trace Facility
  Database Trace Facility
  Data Sharing Diagnosis Aids
  ETO Diagnosis Aids
  Extended Recovery Facility Diagnosis Aids
  MVS Trace Facility

Revision

Reference Information
  Diagnosis Aids
    Data Sharing Diagnosis Aids
    Extended Recovery Facility Diagnosis Aids
  Trace Facilities
    ABC Trace Facility
    Database Trace Facility
    MVS Trace Facility

The organization of the original reference section is usable; however, the sections on trace facilities are mixed with the sections on diagnosis aids. The revised reference section is organized by category. The trace facility sections are first, followed by the diagnosis aid sections.

145

Organize information consistently

Consistency helps users become familiar with the information so they can find what they need with more assurance. When you present information consistently, users learn to predict what information they will find and where they will find it, and they can anticipate what to do with it. If you don't present information consistently, users don't know what to expect.

Organizing information consistently also helps you ensure that your information is complete. Therefore, this guideline is similar to "Use patterns of information to ensure proper coverage" on page 62 in the chapter on completeness.

Users expect information to be predictably organized. A consistent presentation helps users familiar with the information for one product predict correctly how to find information for related products. The organization of a standard document, such as a getting started book or a contextual help window, should follow a similar pattern across related products. For example, if you include tips inside task steps in some help windows and other help windows have tips after task steps, users might fail to notice some of the tips.

Users also expect to find similar sorts of information presented at the same level of detail. For example, if your users must decide between two recovery methods, and for one method you tell them precisely how long it takes, but you omit this information for the other method, your users will be unable to decide on the basis of time.

The following outline is for an introduction to a database product.

Original

> **Retrieving Data**
> **Updating Data**
> **Inserting Data**
> **Deleting Data**
>   Specify Which Data
>   Verify the Data
>   Delete the Data
> **Creating Files**
> **Dropping Files**

Revision

> **Retrieving Data**
> **Updating Data**
> **Inserting Data**
> **Deleting Data**
> **Creating Files**
> **Dropping Files**

The original outline has a section that appears out of proportion to the other information. In the revision, "Deleting Data" is covered at the same overview level as the other topics.

Organize help into discrete topics and types

Users don't like to scroll. Try to keep your help windows short enough so that users don't need to scroll. If that's not possible, try to keep the windows small enough to limit the need for scrolling to the length of one help window (approximately 25 lines). One way to do this is to organize your information into small chunks. Users can link to information only when needed, which saves them from having to view or scroll text that they are not interested in.

A help window might have crucial information on it or a warning to users about an action, but users can miss it if it's hidden from view.

The following help window includes some extraneous text that is probably of little interest to the user who needs task help.

Original

Help

Sending Online Checks

When you send your online checks to the InfoBanker server, InfoBanker processes the checks and sends them to the addresses you specified. Your name and payee account number are also specified on the checks so the payee who receives the check knows which account to credit for the payment.

InfoBanker is connected electronically to certain payees and can send your checks to those payees in one day. Checks to payees that are not connected to InfoBanker's network can take up to four days to send.

To send your online checks:

1. Click **Write Your Checks**. The electronic checkbook opens.
2. In the **Name** field, type the name of the payee. If you specify a name that is not already defined to InfoBanker, the Payee Details window opens so you can define a new payee name, address, and account number.
3. In the **Date** field, type the date you want the check to reach the payee.
4. In the **Amount** field, type the amount of the check.
5. Optional: In the **Memo** field, specify a memo.
6. Click **OK**.
7. Repeat steps 2 through 6 for each check you want to write.

⋮

Revision

```
┌─────────────────────────────────────────────────────────┐
│ ▌ Help                                          □ □ □     │
├─────────────────────────────────────────────────────────┤
│  ┌───────────────────────────────────────────────────┐  │
│  │                                                     │  │
│  │  **Sending Your Online Checks**                     │  │
│  │                                                     │  │
│  │  To send your online checks:                        │  │
│  │                                                     │  │
│  │    1. Click **Write Your Checks**. The electronic   │  │
│  │       checkbook opens.                              │  │
│  │    2. In the **Name** field, type the name of the   │  │
│  │       payee. If you specify a name                  │  │
│  │       that is not already defined to InfoBanker,    │  │
│  │       the Payee Details window                      │  │
│  │       opens so you can define a new payee name,     │  │
│  │       address, and account                          │  │
│  │       number.                                       │  │
│  │    3. In the **Date** field, type the date you      │  │
│  │       want the check to reach the payee.            │  │
│  │       Some restrictions apply.                      │  │
│  │    4. In the **Amount** field, type the amount of   │  │
│  │       the check.                                    │  │
│  │    5. Optional: In the **Memo** field, specify a    │  │
│  │       memo.                                         │  │
│  │    6. Click **OK**.                                 │  │
│  │    7. Repeat steps 2 through 6 for each check you   │  │
│  │       want to write.                                │  │
│  │    8. Click **Send** to send the checks to the      │  │
│  │       server.                                       │  │
│  │                                                     │  │
│  └───────────────────────────────────────────────────┘  │
└─────────────────────────────────────────────────────────┘
```

Because the preliminary text in the original help window takes up space on the window, the eighth step does not fit inside the window. The user might not notice the important eighth step in the task. The revised help window does not contain the extra text; it contains only the information the user needs. The extra information is provided in a link.

You can start chunking your online help by separating task, conceptual, and contextual information into separate help topics. Determine what information users need for each type of help and filter out extraneous information. If users will need more information than what's on the help window, make sure it is available from a button or link.

The following help window contains information about the window, the fields, the tasks, and the concepts.

Original

Help ▢ ▢ ▢

Use this window to schedule a script to run. A script is a series of commands you can create to run InfoProduct functions. After you create the script, you can schedule it to run at any time or at specific intervals. You can create and run a script only if you have the proper authorizations.

To schedule a script:

1. In the Script field, type the name of the script.
2. Select a radio button to specify whether you want to run the script once or at intervals. You can select:

   Once   Runs the script once. Specify the date and time in the Date and Time fields.

   Repeatedly Runs the script at the frequency you specify in the Frequency field. Specify the date and time to begin in the Date and Time fields.

3. Click **OK**.

Fields and Push Buttons

Script	Type the 1- to 8-character name of the existing script.
Once	Select this radio button to run the script once.
Repeatedly	Select this radio button to run the script at intervals.
Frequency	Specify how often (in hours) to run the script. For example, type 12 to run the script every 12 hours.
Date	Specify the date in this format: mmddyyyy
Time	Specify the time in this format: hh:mm:ss, where 0<=h<=23.
OK	Select this push button to save your changes and close the window.
Cancel	Select this push button to undo your changes and close the window.

Related Information

☐ Script scenarios
☐ InfoProduct functions and commands

151

Revision

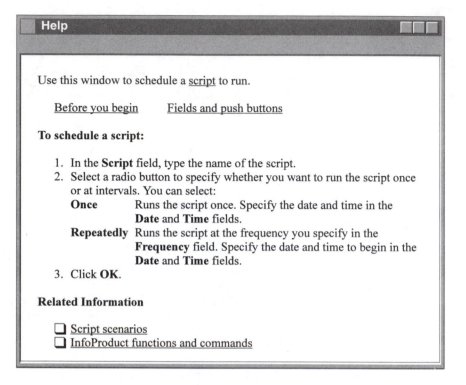

The original help window requires users to scan through the whole help window to locate the information they need. The revised help system shows the information separated by type; users can read the information they need and can skip what they don't need.

There is more than one way to chunk online help. In the revision, the writer decided that help for the window would best serve the user if it focused on the task the user can perform in the window. The other kinds of information are provided by links. In cases where a window is used to perform multiple tasks, additional chunking might be needed.

Emphasize main points, subordinate secondary points

You can use emphasis and subordination to distinguish between main points and supporting information. Users need a way to tell the highways apart from the back roads; they get lost when they can't keep track of the main points.

Emphasizing a main point involves:

Placement

Placing topics or words first is the best way to emphasize a main point: in the heading, in the introduction, in the first sentence of a paragraph, in the first words of a sentence.

Introduction

An introduction should announce to the user why what is coming is important or how it is relevant. Such an orientation places the subsequent information in context and thus makes it easier for users to learn.

Repetition and reinforcement

Repetition keeps the user's mind on the point throughout the presentation. Effective reinforcement includes making a point in more than one way, such as by text and illustration, or by general statement and example.

Detail

Details help emphasize what is important. Provide users with more details on important topics, fewer details on topics that are not as important.

The following paragraph seems to be about paragraphs at first, but is actually trying to make a point about how to use markup tags.

Original

> Paragraphs may have their first lines indented, or not; they may be set to the left margin or indented under headings; they may be separated by one blank line, two blank lines, or none. But they all begin with a tag designating a paragraph. Similarly, a highlighted phrase may be underlined when it is printed on one device, appear in italics when printed on another, and show up in red when displayed on a window. It is still the same kind of element, a highlighted phrase, identified by the same highlighting tag. Thus the generalized markup tag identifies the kind of element a portion of a document is.

First Revision

> The generalized markup tag identifies the kind of element a portion of a document is, not the way it is to be formatted. Paragraphs may be set to the left margin or indented under headings; they may be separated by one blank line, two blank lines, or none. But they all begin with a paragraph tag. Similarly, a highlighted phrase may be underlined when it is printed on one device, appear in italics when printed on another, and show up in red when displayed on a window. It is still the same kind of element, a highlighted phrase, identified by a highlighting tag. Therefore, when marking a portion of a document, ask yourself, "What kind of element is this?" not "How do I want this to look?"

Second Revision

> The generalized markup tag identifies the kind of element a portion of a document is, not the way it is to be formatted. For example:
>
> ❑ Paragraphs are identified with a paragraph tag. They may be set to the left margin or indented under headings; they may be separated by one blank line, two blank lines, or none. But they all begin with a paragraph tag.
>
> ❑ A highlighted phrase is identified by a highlighting tag. It may be underlined when it is printed on one device, appear in italics when printed on another, and show up in red when displayed on a window. It is still the same kind of element, a highlighted phrase.
>
> Therefore, when marking a portion of a document, ask yourself, "What *kind* of element is this?" not "How do I want this to look?"

The first revised paragraph begins with the topic sentence. It uses repetition, contrast, and rephrasing to emphasize the main point. In addition, the second revised paragraph uses a list to set off the examples more clearly and make the information easier to scan. It also uses placement and reinforcement in the list items to keep the focus on the main point.

When you give unwarranted emphasis to secondary information through placement, introduction, repetition, or detail, you make that information seem more important than it is. Though a minor point may belong in the text, elaboration of the point may not.

In the following passage a note is used to call attention to information that is no more pertinent than the other information in the passage.

Original

> You can cancel registrations if you no longer need to copy data or if the registration is erroneous. You can cancel only the registrations you created.
>
> **Note:** Canceling registrations ensures that the InfoBase control tables are properly updated and prevents database errors.

Revision

> You can cancel registrations if you no longer need to copy data or if the registration is erroneous. You can cancel only the registrations you created. Canceling registrations ensures that the InfoBase control tables are properly updated and prevents database errors.

The original passage gives unnecessary emphasis to the statement about the benefits of canceling a registration. That statement is no more important than the other two statements, yet the note gives users the impression that it must be more important.

It's tempting to use notes when you insert new information into previously written documents. However, you'll soon find that your documents have a lot of notes and no flow and that users can't follow your main points. Take the time to fit the new information into the existing structure, or reorganize the information to accommodate the new information if needed. In the revision, the information fits into the original paragraph without any rewriting.

Divide a topic only if it has at least two subtopics

If a topic seems to have only one subheading, it is a good indication that there is an organization problem. If there is only one main thing to say about a topic, there is no need for a subheading. If a topic must be subdivided, there must be more than one subtopic to present.

The following outline shows a chapter with one main subheading.

Original

> **Chapter 8. File Structure**
>   File Structure Table
> **Chapter 9. Troubleshooting**

Revision

> **Chapter 8. File Structure**
> **Chapter 9. Troubleshooting**

The main subheading in the original outline is as long as the chapter. Closer investigation shows that the heading was added to separate the table from the introductory text in the chapter. The heading is not needed, as shown in the revised outline.

A more likely problem is not enough headings at the appropriate level, as shown in the following outline.

Original

> **Data Security**
>   Access
> **Data Integrity**

Revision

> **Data Security**
>   Access to the InfoBase System
>   Access to the InfoBase Database
>   Access to the Data Source System
>   Access to the Data Source Database
> **Data Integrity**

The original outline shows only one subheading for Data Security. In the revision, the writer reorganized the section so there are now four topics under Data Security.

Branch only when helpful to the user

A *branch* can be a link in online information or a cross-reference in a printed book. A branch sends users to remote information. If they need that information, they have to interrupt their reading to follow the branch.

Decisions by a writer on when to provide a branch and when to repeat information affect completeness and retrievability as well as organization. The section "Repeat information only when users will benefit from it" on page 68 deals with this issue from a completeness perspective. The retrievability aspects are dealt with in "Break up text into manageable chunks" on page 170.

In online information, writers should provide navigation aids (such as previous and next buttons) for users without cluttering the help window with unnecessary links. Writers can also structure help windows or Web documents so that links to related topics appear consistently at the bottom or top of the window or on one side of a split window. In addition, users have the flexibility of using the online search facility to look for information of interest.

Add links in online information only when helpful, and use them consistently. Do not provide links to redundant information. Because Web documents can sometimes take several seconds to load, unhelpful or redundant links are especially tiresome to Web users. Also, be sure the content of the linked text conveys the type of information to which the link takes the user. Before taking a link, users should understand, for example, whether the linked-to information defines a term or gives steps in a procedure.

The following help window is cluttered with links inside the main text.

Original

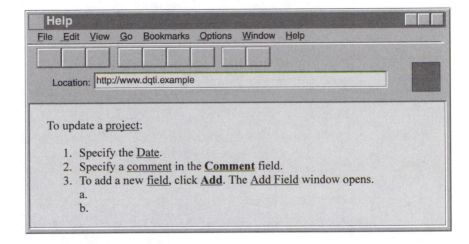

First Revision

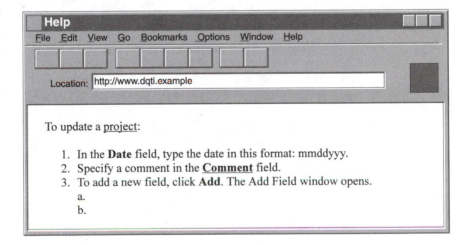

Second Revision

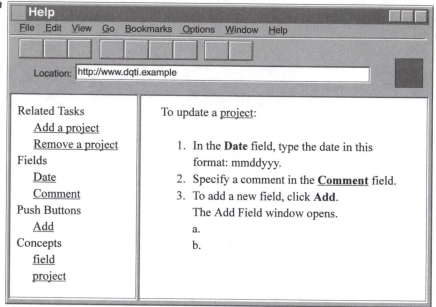

In the original help window, the writer links everything, even information that is redundant. Users of this help system quickly learn that the links (although abundant and consistent) are not helpful. The first revised window uses links only for relevant information. In the second revised window, the links are provided optionally, on the left side of the help window. The second revision also provides links to related tasks. Users can link to these topics if interested.

Users of printed information rarely interrupt their reading to refer to remote information, necessary or not. They resist even a branch that they are told to take, and read on until they discover that, yes, they really can't proceed without taking that branch. They have wasted time trying to go ahead. For example, most users will ignore a reference to a figure that is only as far away as the facing page. But when the figure appears *on the same page*, right after the reference to it, almost all users will read the figure immediately.

When a reference appears in a printed book, there are degrees of remoteness: the reference may be to the facing page, to the other side of the page, to a specific page in the book, to a subject in the same book with no page number specified, to another book closely related to the one in hand, to a book for another product, or to online information.

Some of the branches in the following steps can be avoided by providing a minimal amount of extra information inside the step.

Original

> To add a column:
>
> 1. Fill in the **Name** field. See "Column Names" on page 99 for the syntax.
>
> 2. In the **Data Type** field, specify the data type. See Table 8 on page 53 for a list of valid data types.
>
> 3. In the **Length** field, specify the maximum length for the column. See Table 9 on page 58 for a list of maximum length values for each data type.

Revision

> To add a column:
>
> 1. In the **Name** field, specify a 1- to 8- character column name. Blanks are not allowed.
>
> 2. In the **Data Type** field, specify the data type. Allowable values are integer, decimal, character, LOB, double, date, and time.
>
> 3. In the **Length** field, specify the maximum length for the column. See Table 9 on page 58 for a list of maximum length values for each data type.

The original steps contain three branches, one for each step. In the revision, the writer is able to provide sufficient information inside two of the steps to save users from needing to branch. The third step still requires the users to branch because the information is too bulky to fit inside the step.

The branch in the following passage is to a section on how to use a command during installation.

Original

Administrator	Can authorize other users and can register the data. The administrator is the owner of the user ID that runs the ABCONTROL command during installation. See "ABCONTROL Command" on page 129 for more information about the command.
User	Can enter data into a subset of tables, as authorized by the administrator.

Revision

Administrator	Can authorize other users and can register the data. The administrator is the owner of the user ID that runs the ABCONTROL command during installation.
User	Can enter data into a subset of tables, as authorized by the administrator.

In the original passage, the user is reading about the difference between an administrator and a user. The user doesn't need to know the details about how to use an installation command. The original passage provides the branch in case a user might be immediately interested in that information. The revised example saves most users the trouble of branching to unnecessary information. Any users especially interested in the ABCONTROL command can look it up. It is not necessary to cross-reference a topic every time it is mentioned.

Save your users confusion and wasted time—avoid unnecessary branches.

Reveal how the pieces fit together

When users first encounter a piece of information, they usually want to see it as part of a whole. Like travelers, they need a map both at the beginning of a journey and as their trip progresses to keep their bearings in relation to the destination.

This guideline encompasses a similar guideline in the retrievability chapter, "In introductory sections, reveal the order of topics to come" on page 185. However, this guideline deals with the whole presentation of a document's organization, not just with section introductions.

For books (whether online or printed), users use the following elements as a map: tables of contents, headings, introductions, transitions, and certain graphics.

Because online help is not read linearly, conveying the overall organization to the user is difficult and perhaps unnecessary. However, you can help by providing overview windows that list topics users can link to. Users can return to these windows as necessary to link to other topics. In this way, users get a sense of the structure of the information and can read it linearly if they want to. You can also provide users with information about the kinds of help available (task, conceptual, contextual), so they can better understand how the help is organized.

Users can read Web documents linearly or they can skip around. Users can usually enter a Web site from more than one place, so you should provide explicit information to users about where they are in the Web site and where they can go.

Users keep their bearings by reading transitions, reminders, explanations, examples, and summaries. In online help, users keep their bearings with the help of layered or split windows, help history lists, and push buttons that take them to the previous window. In all these cases, users are verifying their sense of the whole. If they can't verify it or if a piece doesn't fit, something is missing or wrong.

The following chapter introduction provides only a list of subheadings in the chapter.

Original

> This chapter contains:
>
> ❑ Selecting the project
> ❑ Editing the project
> ❑ Scheduling the project
> ❑ Launching the project

Revision

> This chapter explains how to use the sample project provided with InfoProduct. There are four steps involved:
>
> 1. Selecting the project.
> 2. Editing the default values in the project.
> 3. Scheduling the project.
> 4. Launching the project.

The original introduction fails to explain how the subheadings fit together in the chapter. The revised introduction explains that the subheadings are all subtasks of the main task and indicates that they should be done in order.

The following passage shows the end of a section that explains how to install a product.

Original

> 9. Press Enter. InfoProduct is installed.

Revision

> 9. Press Enter. InfoProduct is installed.
>
> You can now configure the settings; see Chapter 3 for steps. If you want to use the tutorial before you configure the settings, see Appendix B.

The original section ends as soon as the product is installed and doesn't point the users to the next place to go in the book. The users must figure out what to do next, if anything. The revised section explains to the users that they can go on to Chapter 3 or use the tutorial now. In some cases, transitions like this are unnecessary and could annoy users. To determine whether transitions between sections are helpful and warranted, you need to know your audience.

The following Web page doesn't tell the user what product the page supports and doesn't provide navigational aids to the product's home page, company page, or a map of the Web site.

Original

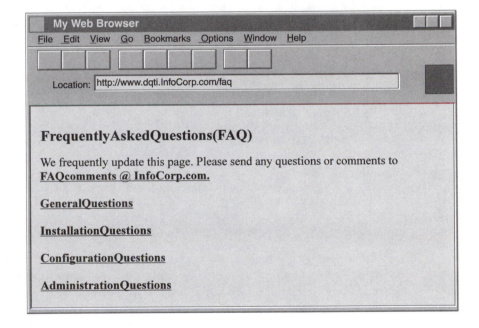

Revision

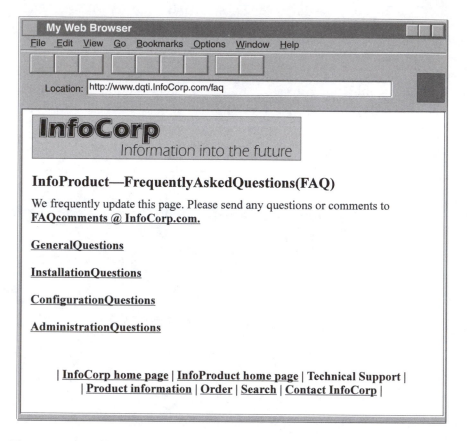

The original Web page is an "orphaned" Web page. Users who come across this page can't tell from the title which product it supports. In addition, they can't link to the product's home page to find out more about the space.

The revised Web page provides the product's name in the title so users know which FAQ they are reading. This page also provides navigational aids so users can explore the other pages in the Web site. The product home page provides links to the other pages about the product, the company home page provides links to pages for other products the company sells, and the search facility allows the users to search the Web site directly from the FAQ page.

In sum

Use the guidelines in this chapter to ensure that technical information is organized well. Refer to the examples in the chapter for practical applications of these guidelines.

When you review technical information for organization, you can use this checklist in two ways:

- ❏ As a reminder of what to look for, to ensure a thorough review
- ❏ As an evaluation tool, to determine the quality of the information

You can apply the quality rating in the third column of the checklist to the guideline as a whole. Judging by the number and severity of items you found, decide how the information rates on each guideline for this quality characteristic. You can then add your findings to "Quality Checklist" on page 269, which covers all the quality characteristics.

Although the guidelines are intended to cover all areas for this quality characteristic, you might find additional items to add to the list for a guideline.

Guidelines for organization	Items to look for	Quality rating
Organize guidance information sequentially.	• Task steps are presented in order of use. • Sufficient conceptual information is provided to begin a task.	1 2 3 4 5
Organize reference information logically.	• Order of information is logical.	1 2 3 4 5
Organize information consistently.	• Sequence of information is consistent. • Amount of detail is consistent.	1 2 3 4 5
Organize help into discrete topics and types.	• Help windows do not require excessive scrolling. • Help topics are separated by type.	1 2 3 4 5
Emphasize main points, subordinate secondary points.	• Paragraphs are presented to emphasize main points. • Heading levels are appropriate. • Use of notes to call attention is appropriate.	1 2 3 4 5
Divide a topic only if it has at least two subtopics.	• Topics with subtopics have at least two subtopics.	1 2 3 4 5
Branch only when helpful to the user.	• Branches are avoided by providing sufficient information in context, where appropriate. • There are no unnecessary branches. • Cross-references do not loop. • Linking is appropriate.	1 2 3 4 5
Reveal how the pieces fit together.	• Hierarchy of topics is apparent. • Transitions are provided as needed. • Organization of Web site is clear.	1 2 3 4 5

Note: The scale for the quality rating goes from very satisfied (1) to very dissatisfied (5).

Chapter 9

Retrievability

Information with good retrievability enables users to find what they need quickly and easily. Many elements contribute to good retrievability: obvious ones like the table of contents, index, links, and headings, and not so obvious ones like highlighting, revision markers, icons, and margin graphics. These elements and others like them are *entry points*—signposts that orient and direct users so they can find the information they need.

To develop information with good retrievability, follow these guidelines:

❑ **Break up text into manageable chunks.**

❑ **Stock the index with entries that users expect.**

❑ **Make sure the index is complete and correct.**

❑ **Make linked-to information easy to find on the target help window or page.**

❑ **In introductory sections, reveal the order of topics to come.**

❑ **Use an appropriate level of detail in a table of contents.**

❑ **Make key terms easy to find.**

Break up text into manageable chunks

Few things in complex technical information are more discouraging than large blocks of text, unbroken by headings, graphics, or other visual aids. In general, limit blocks of text to no more than 6 lines in online information and 12 lines in printed information. (This guideline and others like it in this book are ballpark estimates based on experience, not precise rules.)

Headings are the usual way to break up text. Lists and short paragraphs also provide major entry points, as shown in the following pair of examples:

Original

> Because this is the first dimension you are creating for your plan, the InfoWrite editor is empty, ready for you to type your definitions. First, type a name for the dimension in the **Dimension** field. The name can be up to 12 characters, including uppercase or lowercase letters, but must contain no spaces. The first character must be alphabetic. Next, in the **Level** field, type the number of the highest level in the dimension hierarchy. The highest level is the level at the top of the dimension hierarchy. It has the lowest number in the dimension definition. It is good practice to leave gaps between the level numbers so that intermediate levels can be added later if they are needed. For example, in a dimension that has four levels, use level 10 as the highest, then levels 20, 30, and 40 as the next levels. Type the name of the element that is at this level in the **Contents** field. The name must be unique and can have up to 24 characters, including uppercase and lowercase letters and spaces. Press Enter to add it to the list of dimension elements.

First Revision

Creating a dimension

Because this is the first dimension you are creating for your plan, the InfoWrite editor is empty, ready for you to type your definitions.

To create a dimension:

1. In the **Dimension** field, type a name for the dimension.

   Rules for the dimension name: The name can be up to 12 characters, including uppercase or lowercase letters, but must contain no spaces. The first character must be alphabetic.

2. In the **Level** field, type the number of the highest level in the dimension hierarchy.

   About dimension levels: The highest level is the level at the top of the dimension hierarchy. It has the lowest number in the dimension definition.

   Tip: Leave gaps between the level numbers. You can then add intermediate numbers later if they are needed.

   For example, in a dimension that has four levels, use level 10 as the highest, then levels 20, 30, and 40 as the next levels.

3. In the **Contents** field, type the name of the element that is at this level.

   Rules for the element name: The name must be unique and can have up to 24 characters, including uppercase and lowercase letters and spaces.

4. Press Enter. The new element name is added to the list of dimension elements.

In the original text, several kinds of information are run together in one overwhelming paragraph. On close examination, you can find steps for a procedure (with a tip and example), rules for naming, and conceptual information.

The revised text first adds a heading for the primary topic, which is a task. It then shows the task steps by using an ordered list, and separates the naming rules and conceptual information by using subheadings. The tip and example are set off as separate paragraphs.

If you were breaking up this information for online presentation, you might choose to link to the reference and conceptual information, as in the following example:

Second Revision

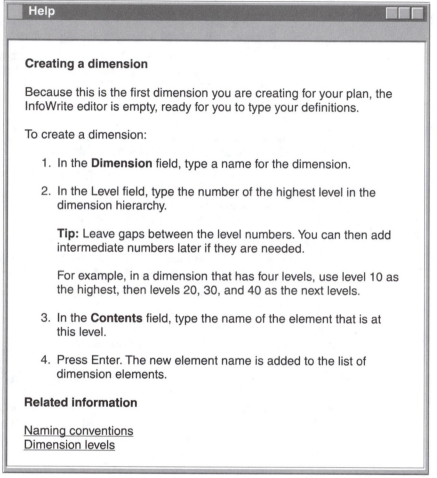

Help

Creating a dimension

Because this is the first dimension you are creating for your plan, the InfoWrite editor is empty, ready for you to type your definitions.

To create a dimension:

1. In the **Dimension** field, type a name for the dimension.

2. In the Level field, type the number of the highest level in the dimension hierarchy.

   Tip: Leave gaps between the level numbers. You can then add intermediate numbers later if they are needed.

   For example, in a dimension that has four levels, use level 10 as the highest, then levels 20, 30, and 40 as the next levels.

3. In the **Contents** field, type the name of the element that is at this level.

4. Press Enter. The new element name is added to the list of dimension elements.

Related information

Naming conventions
Dimension levels

The linked-to information on naming conventions would have the rules for dimension names and element names. It would probably be a common help window, linked to from many other procedures, and might contain a full set of rules. The linked-to information on dimension levels would describe the term and perhaps include more information about the levels. If no more information would be useful to users, a link to a glossary definition of *dimension hierarchy* might replace the later link. When information moves to other help windows, more possibilities open up for ways to present it, because it no longer has to fit in with surrounding information that might be tangential.

Headings are the most common way to break up information, but just because some headings are good doesn't mean that more are better. Not only do they distract from each other, but they disrupt the organization and flow of the information, particularly when the heading level (level of subordination) changes frequently. Compare the following two examples:

Original

> **SUMMARY OF INFOMANAGER REPORTS**
>
> InfoManager generates different kinds of reports at each stage in the process of restructuring your program: conversion, analysis and generation.
>
> **CONVERSION MODE REPORTS**
>
> **Input Report**
>
> Listing of the input program (with each line numbered)
>
> **Output Report**
>
> Listing of the output program (with each line numbered)
>
> **ANALYSIS MODE REPORTS**
>
> In Analysis Mode, InfoManager produces two reports and appends to a third one. The three reports are:
>
> **Input Report**
>
> Listing of the input program (with each line numbered)
>
> **Reengineering Report**
>
> Detailed analysis of the logic in the input program, and complexity metrics for the input program
>
> **Complexity Metrics Summary Report**
>
> Summary of the complexity metrics of all programs that you have analyzed and structured
>
> **GENERATION MODE REPORTS**
>
> In Generation Mode, InfoManager produces two reports and appends to a third one. The three reports are:
>
> **Input Report**
>
> Listing of the input program (with each line numbered)
>
> **Output Report**
>
> Listing of the output program (with each line numbered)
>
> **Reengineering Report**
>
> Structure charts of the output program, advice to help modularize the output program, and sections describing properties of the output program

Revision

Summary of InfoManager Reports

InfoManager generates different kinds of reports at each stage in the process of restructuring your program: conversion, analysis, and generation.

Conversion Mode Reports

Input Report
Listing of the input program (with each line numbered)

Output Report
Listing of the output program (with each line numbered)

Analysis Mode Reports

In Analysis Mode, InfoManager produces two reports and appends to a third one. The three reports are:

Input Report
Listing of the input program (with each line numbered)

Reengineering Report
Detailed analysis of the logic in the input program, and complexity metrics for the input program

Complexity Metrics Summary Report
Summary of the complexity metrics of all programs that you have analyzed and structured

Generation Mode Reports

In Generation Mode, InfoManager produces two reports and appends to a third one. The three reports are:

Input Report
Listing of the input program (with each line numbered)

Output Report
Listing of the output program (with each line numbered)

Reengineering Report
Structure charts of the output program, advice to help modularize the output program, and sections describing properties of the output program

---

In the original text, too many headings make it hard to understand how the reports relate to the three modes of the program. In the revised text, the report names have been made part of the text column. The relationship between the program modes and the different reports is clear at a glance.

In an online presentation of the same information, you might create an overview help window with links to more specific information, as in the following example:

Second Revision

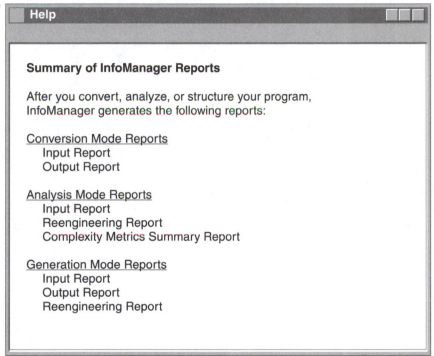

From this overview help window, users select the link if they want more information. The subwindows, however, should provide enough useful information to make the link worth going to.

You need to decide whether information is easier to retrieve if it is on the same help window or on a subwindow. It is usually easier to retrieve on a subwindow if the original help window would be long and the user would have to scroll more than approximately 25 lines. When making this decision, consider also the organization guidelines "Branch only when helpful to the user" on page 158 and "Organize help into discrete topics and types" on page 148.

Stock the index with entries that users expect

In online and printed documents, users often go to the index first when looking for information. Technical writers need to predict what information users will look for, and what words they might expect as pointers to that information.

Verbs can be effective index entries, especially when they are specific and describe a user task, such as "copying," "installing," or "searching." However, a common mistake in indexing is to use generic verbs followed by nouns or adjectives as secondary entries, as in the following example from a printed index:

Original

```
using
  CGI  105-115
  data controls  142
  forms  93
  HTML  9
  perl  105
```

Revision

Some of the verb-noun combinations in the original excerpt may be used as headings in the information, but that doesn't necessarily make them good index entries. Users are more likely to look for a specific noun or verb instead of a generic verb when using an index.

In general, use specific terms and avoid generic ones (like "using") when creating an index. Some words can be specific or generic, depending on how they are used. "Examples" can be a good primary index entry if you have no more than a few dozen examples in your document. But it's too generic if you have hundreds of examples, and in that case you're better off indexing your examples under the specific topic they apply to. Other words that can be specific or generic depending on context include "creating," "updating," "commands," "messages," and "text."

The words or phrases users think of might not be the same ones used in the information, and not all users think alike, even about the same topic or task. Therefore, an index in a printed book must contain synonyms and variations for its entries. In online information, synonyms and variations can also be useful, but too many of them can overload the index and cause too many hits when you search the index for a given word, as shown in the following excerpt from an online index:

Original

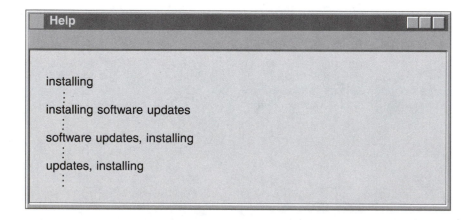

Revision

In the original excerpt, searching on "installing" will generate four hits and searching on "software updates" will generate two hits, with all of these hits pointing to the same place.

In the revised excerpt, users will find the entry whether they search on "software updates," "installing," or "updates," and so the single entry is enough.

Make sure the index is complete and correct

An index needs to have entries for every important task and topic covered in the information. And it needs to be correct in the sense of adhering to indexing guidelines that will make your index entries consistent and easy to use. Below are some indexing guidelines to ensure that your index is complete and correct.

Guidelines for online and printed information

❑ Index every task, concept, and component or object.

❑ Start every index entry with a specific noun or a specific verb (task). If necessary, modify the noun or verb to make it more specific. Whether you put the modifier before or after the noun or verb depends on how users would probably look up the entry.

❑ If you use secondary or tertiary entries, put at least two of them at each level.

❑ Avoid index entries that start with a generic term that users are unlikely to look up, such as "changing," "managing," "tasks," or "using."

Guidelines for online information only

❑ For online help, include at least one index entry for every major help window. (Smaller subordinate help windows often do not need index entries because they make sense only when linked to from the parent help window.)

❑ When including synonyms and variations of your index entries, do so sparingly, and consider the search engine that will be used.

Guidelines for printed information only

❑ Include approximately one page of index entries for every 20 pages of text.

❑ In each index entry, put page numbers on only one level.

❑ If an entry has page numbers, it should have no more than two.

❑ Include plenty of synonyms and variations of your index entries.

The following examples from a printed index illustrate the difference between covering a topic with a single entry and covering it with variations in different parts of the index.

Original

```
help
   command  22
   general  18
   online  31
   reference  38
```

Revision

```
commands
   HELP  22
   .
   .
   .
general help  18
   .
   .
   .
HELP command  22
help
   general  18
   online  31
   reference  38
   .
   .
   .
online help  31
   .
   .
   .
reference help  38
```

The original excerpt gives entries for "help" in only one place in the index. In the revised excerpt, variations of "help" occur throughout the index, in case users might look someplace other than the "help" entry. In addition, the revised excerpt clarifies that the original subentry "command" is actually for a command named HELP.

As mentioned on page page 178, it's possible to have too many index entry variations, particularly in an online index. And any index can become over-loaded with ineffective entries. As explained in "Completeness" on page 49, completeness in technical writing means neither too much nor too little information, but instead, just the amount that users need to complete their tasks. Although indexes in technical information are occasionally too long, it's far more common for them to be too short, often because indexing is left until the end of the project, when deadlines are pressing. The cure for this problem is to make indexing part of your daily writing process, using the guidelines here to help make your index a good one.

Indexing is a complex subject—people even make a living as professional indexers. For references to more detailed information on indexing, see "Bib-liography" on page 287, especially the section "Easy to Find" on page 290.

Make linked-to information easy to find on the target help window or page

To make your information retrievable, you not only need to provide a good index and arrange the information appropriately on the help help window or printed page; you also need to anticipate what piece of information users will be looking for when they get to the help window or page. You need to consider how users might branch to a given help window or page.

For example, a user might get to a help window from the index or table of contents (if there is one), by linking from another help window, or by a context-sensitive link from the product. In a printed book, a user might get to a page from the index, the table of contents, or a cross-reference. In both cases, you need to make the linked-to information stand out on the target help window or page.

If your online help system branches to the top of a help window instead of to a specific place within the help window, then put the linked-to information in the title or first sentence of the help window. If this placement is not feasible, highlight the linked-to information on the help window. For printed information, mark the linked-to information with a heading, icon, or appropriate highlighting.

For Web pages, consider the most likely sources of links into your page. A user might link from other pages within your Web site, from other pages controlled by your organization, from an application, or from the Internet. In each case, try to anticipate what information users will be looking for, and then use highlighting, color, graphics, or a heading to make that information stand out on your Web page.

Look at the following example of a Web help page that a user can get to after searching the help index for "changing fonts":

Original

My Web Browser

File   Edit   View   Go   Bookmarks   Options   Window   Help

Location: http://www.dqti.examples

Changing fonts and colors

To see options affecting fonts and colors in general, choose **Options|General**. The dialog box contains tabs to panel settings.

For options affecting the fonts and colors of mail and news, choose **Options|Mail and News**.

On Windows and Macintosh, you can select colors for links, text, and background in the **Colors** panel.

Click the **Custom** check boxes.
Press the **Choose Color** buttons (on Macintosh, click the colored boxes).

If the check box is unchecked, the default settings are:

Unfollowed links	Blue
Followed links	Purple
Text	Black
Background	White

For background, you can also choose an image file.

On Windows and UNIX, the **Images** panel lets you choose how to display an image's colors to most closely match the computer's available colors.

In the **Fonts** panel, a set of menus lets you choose the font and font size for each of the two types of fonts that pages use to display text:

Proportional	Used for most text
Fixed	Used for text in editable fields and certain paragraphs preformatted by the author of a page

183

Revision

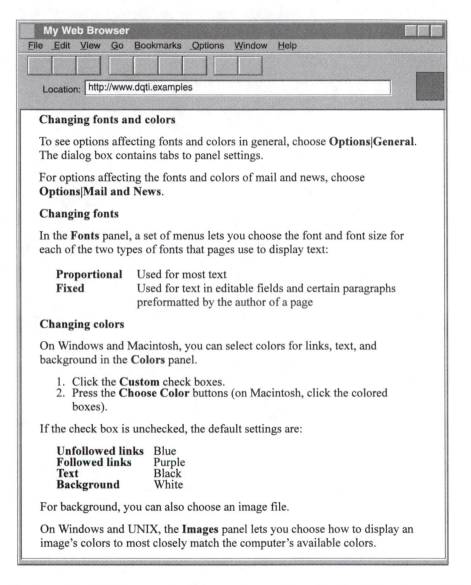

Changing fonts and colors

To see options affecting fonts and colors in general, choose **Options|General**. The dialog box contains tabs to panel settings.

For options affecting the fonts and colors of mail and news, choose **Options|Mail and News**.

Changing fonts

In the **Fonts** panel, a set of menus lets you choose the font and font size for each of the two types of fonts that pages use to display text:

Proportional	Used for most text
Fixed	Used for text in editable fields and certain paragraphs preformatted by the author of a page

Changing colors

On Windows and Macintosh, you can select colors for links, text, and background in the **Colors** panel.

1. Click the **Custom** check boxes.
2. Press the **Choose Color** buttons (on Macintosh, click the colored boxes).

If the check box is unchecked, the default settings are:

Unfollowed links	Blue
Followed links	Purple
Text	Black
Background	White

For background, you can also choose an image file.

On Windows and UNIX, the **Images** panel lets you choose how to display an image's colors to most closely match the computer's available colors.

In the original Web page, the information on changing fonts is at the end. In the revised version, headings guide users to the information they're looking for. Also, the order of sections has been changed so that it corresponds with the original heading.

In introductory sections, reveal the order of topics to come

Use introductory sections to describe the purpose and content of the information that follows. You can also use introductions to describe subtopics and show their relationship to one another. When you list subtopics, make their wording and order match the actual subtopics. Compare the two introductions below:

Original

> **Chapter 1. Installing InfoManager**
>
> This chapter describes the installation procedure for InfoManager on a client workstation.

Revision

> **Chapter 1. Installing InfoManager**
>
> This chapter shows you how to install InfoManager on a client workstation. It also describes the prerequisite hardware and software, and shows you how to configure it for your system, and how to customize its user interface according to your preferences. This chapter contains the following sections:
>
> ❏ Hardware requirements
> ❏ Software requirements
> ❏ Preparing to install InfoManager
> ❏ Installation steps
> ❏ Configuring InfoManager
>
> Customizing the InfoManager user interface

The original introduction to the chapter is too brief, and doesn't preview the topics covered in the chapter. The revised introduction describes the purpose of the chapter, and gives a better description of what it contains. The list of sections in the chapter shows how it is organized, prepares users for what's ahead, and helps them find specific subtopics.

Web pages and help windows are usually small enough not to require an introduction. However, high-level Web pages and help windows that link to many subordinate locations often act as an introduction and include a list of subtopics. This list is usually also a list of links. Some subordinate Web pages and help windows may also need introductions, especially if the page or help window contains a list of tasks. Although users can access items in the list in any order they want, the list should reflect an appropriate order, such as a time sequence or order of importance.

Use an appropriate level of detail in a table of contents

A common mistake in technical information is to put every, or almost every, heading in the information into the table of contents. This practice usually produces an over-complete table of contents that makes individual topics harder to find, and hides rather than reveals the organization of the information.

For online information, the table of contents should include every major help window, but not smaller help windows and subwindows. Include tasks, but don't put window titles in the table of contents for the help. A user looking for help on a specific window is probably looking at that window at the time, and can simply ask for help from the window.

For printed information, use about one table of contents page for every 50 pages of text. For long books (more than 400 pages), a ratio closer to one table of contents page for every 100 pages of text may be more appropriate.

You can reduce the size of the table of contents by limiting the number of heading levels, as shown in the pair of examples below:

The original table of contents shows four levels of headings—probably more detail than a user needs when scanning the contents. In the revised table of contents, three levels are shown, giving the major divisions of the book and the major tasks. This is an appropriate level of detail. Showing only two levels would not give users enough detail to find the information they are looking for.

Make key terms easy to find

Key words and phrases should stand out to attract attention, especially when they are being used for the first time or defined in the text. After users locate a term in the index and go to the help window or page it points to, they still need to find the relevant paragraph or sentence. The right kinds of highlighting and structure make this step easier, as shown in the following pair of examples.

Original

Here are the new features in this version: (1) **long lines**—Version 3 supported up to 255 characters per line, but Version 4 supports up to 1600 bytes (in effect unlimited); (2) **drag and drop** of files and marked text between edit windows and between edit windows and desktop; (3) **fast sort**—much faster than Version 3, with no limit on the amount that can be sorted; (4) **extended grep** adds alternation, grouping, and macros to the standard grep search.

Revision

Here is a list of the new features in this version:

Long lines	Version 3 supports up to 255 characters per line. Version 4 supports lines up to 1600 bytes, but in effect supports unlimited length lines.
Drag and drop	Move files and marked text between edit windows, or between edit windows and desktop.
Fast sort	Much faster than Version 3, with no limit on the amount that can be sorted.
Extended grep	Adds alternation, grouping, and macros to the standard grep search.

In the original text, it's difficult to locate a specific feature, such as fast sort. In the revised text, the list is formatted so that users can easily find what they're looking for. Another method of making the same information more retrievable is to put it in a table, with headings to indicate the type of feature and its function or how it's been improved.

When writing help or Web information, take into account the type of search tool that will be used. Some search tools may search only headings and defined "keywords," while others may do a full text search but *not* search text in headings. Make sure that your search tool will locate all of the key terms that you've defined.

Although highlighting is a good way to make your key terms stand out, excessive highlighting does more harm than good. Too many highlighted phrases compete for attention and defeat the purpose. And too many different kinds of highlighting (bold, color, italics, underlining) confuse readers instead of directing them to your key terms and concepts. Compare the two examples below:

Original

> A database can be classified into one of two groups based on the method used to store data in it. HSAM, SHSAM, HISAM, and SHISAM databases use the **sequential** method. With this method, the **hierarchic** sequence of segments in the database is maintained by putting segments in storage locations that are **physically adjacent** to each other. HDAM, HIDAM, MSDB, and DEDB databases use the **direct** method of storing data. With this method, the hierarchic sequence of segments is maintained by putting **direct-address** pointers in each segment's prefix.

Revision

> A database can be classified into one of two groups based on the method used to store data in it: sequential or direct.
>
> **Sequential method**   HSAM, SHSAM, HISAM, and SHISAM databases use the sequential method. With this method, the hierarchic sequence of segments in the database is maintained by putting segments in storage locations that are physically adjacent to each other.
>
> **Direct method**   HDAM, HIDAM, MSDB, and DEDB databases use the direct method of storing data. With this method, the hierarchic sequence of segments is maintained by putting direct-access pointers in each segment's prefix.

The original text shows a paragraph in which several terms are highlighted, using two different kinds of highlighting. Yet the first statement sets the topic, and the content defines the two parts of the topic. So the revised text uses a list and highlighting to emphasize the topic and make the definitions of the two new terms easy to find. The other highlighted terms in the original text are defined in context but are secondary to the main topic, so they are not highlighted in the revised text.

In sum

Use the guidelines in this chapter to ensure that your technical information is retrievable. Refer to the examples in the chapter for practical applications of these guidelines.

When you review technical information for retrievability, you can use this checklist in two ways:

❑ As a reminder of what to look for, to ensure a thorough review
❑ As an evaluation tool, to determine the quality of the information

You can apply the quality rating in the third column of the checklist to the guideline as a whole. Judging by the number and severity of items you found, decide how the information rates on each guideline for this quality characteristic. You can then add your findings to "Quality Checklist" on page 269, which covers all the quality characteristics.

Although the guidelines are intended to cover all areas for this quality characteristic, you might find additional items to add to the list for a guideline.

Guidelines for retrievability	Items to look for	Quality rating
Break up text into manageable chunks.	• Online paragraphs are shorter than 6 lines. • Printed paragraphs are shorter than 12 lines. • The number of headings is appropriate.	1 2 3 4 5
Stock the index with entries that users expect.	• Index entries are specific. • Variations and synonyms for index entries are indexed. • Online indexes have only a few variations and synonyms.	1 2 3 4 5
Make sure the index is complete and correct.	• Every task, concept, and component is indexed. • The index exceeds the minimum length guideline. • Wherever secondary or tertiary entries are used, there are at least two of them. • Entries in printed indexes have page numbers on only one level. • Entries in printed indexes have no more than two page numbers.	1 2 3 4 5
Make linked-to information easy to find on the target help window or page.	• Linked-to information is highlighted or in the first sentence.	1 2 3 4 5
In introductory sections, reveal the order of topics to come.	• Web pages and help windows have introductions when appropriate. • Printed sections have introductions. • Introductions contain lists of subtopics when appropriate. • Lists of subtopics have the same order and wording as the actual subtopics.	1 2 3 4 5
Use an appropriate level of detail in a table of contents.	• Online tables of contents include all tasks and major help windows. • Printed tables of contents follow the length guidelines.	1 2 3 4 5

Guidelines for retrievability	Items to look for	Quality rating
Make key terms easy to find.	• Key terms and definitions are appropriately highlighted. • Overall, the amount of highlighting is appropriate. • Only a few (2-3) different kinds of highlighting are used.	1 2 3 4 5

Note: The scale for the quality rating goes from very satisfied (1) to very dissatisfied (5).

Developing Quality Technical Information

Chapter 10

Visual Effectiveness

Visual effectiveness is a measure of how the appearance of information affects the ease with which users can find, understand, and use it.

The appearance of technical information influences, to a greater or lesser degree, all of the other quality characteristics. Visual elements can help task orientation by emphasizing the sequence of task steps. They can support accuracy by correctly depicting facts and their interrelationships. They can be used to complete a description or explanation and to clarify information that might be confusing or too complex if conveyed in words alone. Visual elements are the principal tools for lending concreteness to information, helping facts "come alive." They can set the tone of information and reinforce a consistent style. Visual elements can make important information easier to find, and can reinforce its organization.

The ever-increasing power, accessibility, and interconnectivity of computers greatly increases the variety of information delivery media available to us. Most of these media offer a richness of graphical capabilities that are not available in the print media:

- Bright, user-modifiable interfaces and color palettes
- Increasingly easy-to-use software for creating and manipulating images
- Easy integration of images, animation, video, and sound with text
- World Wide Web browsers that deliver information quickly and seamlessly

Such rich and varied graphical media and methods offer potential for either enhancing or diminishing the quality of technical information; you must ensure the former.

The initial goal of your visual presentation should be to attract and encourage users to begin accessing your information, and then to help motivate them to continue reading. Users are motivated when they perceive a reasonable chance of success at their task. Effective use of graphical elements can help users perceive that chance of success and make their search for the information they need more interesting, effective, and fun.

To make information visually effective, follow these guidelines:

❏ **Balance the amount and placement of visual elements.**
❏ **Use graphics that are meaningful and appropriate.**
❏ **Choose illustrations that complement the text.**
❏ **Present textual elements in a legible size and font.**
❏ **Use visual elements for emphasis.**
❏ **Use visual elements logically and consistently.**
❏ **Use color and shading discreetly and significantly.**
❏ **Use visual cues to help users find what they need.**

Balance the amount and placement of visual elements

Everything that the user can see on the window or page contributes to or detracts from the information's visual effectiveness:

Layout
Color of background, text, and graphics and contrast between them
Typeface and type size
Illustrations and icons
Tables, charts, and examples
Tabs
Line length
Paragraph length
Highlighting
Headings
Lists
Spacing
Overall information density
Use of white space

Users are easily overwhelmed and discouraged by large blocks of text in technical information. Visually varied elements can help users gather information more easily and confidently. Lists, tables, illustrations, examples, and other visual elements, interspersed among paragraphs of text, provide users with a chance to pause to evaluate and absorb before moving on. Such elements also make information more accessible, interesting, and memorable.

White space can also offer a place for the eye to rest and can make a window, page, or two-page spread appear less dense and intimidating. Be sure, though, that extra white space does not interrupt the flow of information on the page or window; such an interruption can imply to the user that something is missing.

The following page has many quality problems. Its appearance is so dense and unvarying that it becomes a barrier to the user rather than a help.

Original

The most common storage shortage problems involve KJH. MCAT uses large amounts of KJH for its control blocks and buffers containing data that is being sent around the network. This problem can be due to a variety of causes. For example, if one application is flooding another with data, and the second application is unable to receive the data and process it at an adequate rate, then the buffers build up in MCAT storage. This situation can be avoided by using session pacing.

If MCAT is unable to get enough storage to issue a message, then the normal storage shortage message is accompanied by an IST999E message.

FGHMP and QFRDT: The Primary return code (FGHMP) and secondary return code (QFRDT) are both given to DDF when an APPCCMD macro has completed. On occasion, these codes may indicate that there is a storage shortage in MCAT. For example, if FGHMP is x'0037' and QFRDT is x'0000', then this indicates a storage shortage while MCAT was receiving data or sending a pacing response. A FGHMP of x'0093' with QFRDT of x'0000' indicates there is a temporary storage shortage while sending data. Usually this return code means that the send request has temporarily depleted the buffer pool to such an extent that the pool must be expanded. The expansion had not occurred before the completion of the APPCCMD macro.

SNA sense code: Some SNA sense codes indicate there may be a storage shortage also. For example, a user might be accessing data from the remote database, and receive '037C0000'. Checking this sense code in the manual indicates that there is a permanent insufficient resource condition. This resource could be storage. Other sense codes, such as '300A000' indicate a storage type problem, but not necessarily a storage shortage.

Errors: There are a series of PJL errors which indicate storage shortage problems. For example, ERROR373 and ERROR30A. These are uncommon in MCAT.

Hangs: Depending on the storage shortage and the processing that is occurring, the storage shortage could manifest itself in a hang situation. For example, if a virtual route becomes blocked due to storage shortages, then all the sessions that had been using that session hangs until the storage shortage is relieved and the virtual route becomes open again. When any of these indications of a storage problem is received, the following steps can be used to find out more information about the shortage:

Determine the area of storage shortage. This is important, as the MCAT display command has information about the MCAT KJH usage. This does not help diagnosis if the storage shortage is in MCAT private. However, perhaps KJH usage should probably be checked anyway.

Display buffer usage: If the storage shortage has occurred in one of the KJH subpools, then a "P SET,DCVRF" command can be used to determine the amount of KJH storage being used by MCAT. Usually the buffer use display gives a good dea of which MCAT pool is causing the storage shortage.

Monitor buffer usage: When looking at a buffer shortage, it is often helpful to know whether the onset of the problem was gradual or immediate. If regular buffer usage displays are done, then gradual increases in buffer use can be seen. These gradual increases may take days to manifest themselves into storage shortage problems. In fact, if MCAT is taken down regularly, the storage shortage symptom may never been seen.

Another benefit of regular monitoring of the buffers is that when a problem does occur "normal" buffer usage for that host is known, so some comparison of the buffer values can be done.

If the onset of the buffer shortage is very fast, then check the system console (or log), looking for some event that has triggered this problem. This could be virtually anything. For example, an BJX has a problem and large amounts of data that was heading out onto the network is now

Revision

Table 1. Indicators of Storage Shortage Problems

Indicator	Problem	Notes
KJH	If one application is flooding another with data and the second application is unable to receive the data and process it at an adequate rate, the buffers build up in MCAT storage.	This situation can be avoided by using session pacing.
IST999E message	MCAT is unable to get enough storage to issue a message	Accompanies the normal storage shortage message
FGHMP=x'0037' with QFRDT=x'0000'	A storage shortage while MCAT was receiving data or sending a pacing response.	Given to DDF when an APPCCMD macro has completed
FGHMP=x'0093' with QFRDT=x'0000'	A storage shortage while sending data. Usually means that the send request has temporarily depleted the buffer pool to such an extent that the pool must be expanded, and the expansion has not occurred before the completion of the APPCCMD macro.	Given to DDF when an APPCCMD macro has completed
SNA sense code x'037C0000'	Indicates a permanent insufficient resource that could be storage	
SNA sense code x'300A0000'	Indicates a storage type problem, but not necessarily a storage shortage.	
PJL ERROR373 or ERROR30A	Indicate storage shortage problems but are uncommon in MCAT.	
Hangs	All the sessions using a specific session as a virtual route might hang if the virtual route becomes blocked because of storage shortages	The hang can last until the shortage is relieved and the virtual route reopens.

Pinpointing the Shortage

When any of these indications of a storage problem is received, the following steps can be used to find out more information about the shortage:

1. Determine the area of storage shortage.

   This is important, as the MCAT display command has information about the MCAT KJH usage. This does not help diagnosis if the storage shortage is in MCAT private. However, KJH usage should probably be checked anyway.

2. Display buffer usage.

   If the storage shortage has occurred in one of the KJH subpools, then a "P SET,DCVRF" command can be used to determine the amount of KJH storage being used by MCAT. Usually the buffer use display gives a good idea of which MCAT pool is causing the storage shortage.

3. Monitor buffer usage.

   When looking at a buffer shortage, it is often helpful to know whether the onset of the problem was gradual or immediate. If regular buffer usage displays are done, then gradual increa-

ses in buffer use can be seen. These gradual increases may take days to manifest themselves into storage shortage problems. In fact, if MCAT is taken down regularly, the storage shortage symptom may never been seen.

Another benefit of regular monitoring of the buffers is that when a problem does occur, "normal" buffer usage for that host is known, so some comparison of the buffer values can be done.

4. Check the system console log.

   If the onset of the buffer shortage is very fast, look for some event that has triggered this problem.

   This could be virtually anything. For example, a BJX has a problem and large amounts of data that was heading out onto the network is now caught in MCAT while recovery of the BJX is attempted.

5. Request a dump.

   To finally determine the cause of the problem, a dump is usually necessary. When requesting a dump, you can limit its output by specifying the

The original page offers users no incentive to approach and read it. There is little variation in the density of information, no clue to its organization or to the relative importance of the paragraphs. Nor are there places where the user can pause.

In the revised page, the information has structure and organization. Reference information is in a table, and task steps are in an ordered list. Even a cursory glance at the page now gives users a clear idea of how to approach the information.

Although the page is still full, the varied elements, rules, headings, and changes in density help users pause to absorb manageable chunks of the information. Users can then more easily find where to resume reading.

Use graphics that are meaningful and appropriate

Effective graphics are an integral part of technical information. They can replace descriptive text or supplement it to clarify and enliven it. However, graphics that are merely decorative and are unrelated to the text distract and confuse users and can actually impair their understanding of the information.

Ensure that each illustration accurately depicts the object, concept, or function it is designed to illustrate, and that it does so as simply as possible. Users naturally look at parts of the window or page that contain something other than text. If you use graphics, make looking at them worth users' time; give users accurate information that they can quickly absorb and use.

Illustrate difficult concepts

Carefully choose what you illustrate. Difficult concepts probably offer the best opportunity for using meaningful graphics that are worth the user's time to look at. The following pair of passages deal with a difficult concept.

Original

> ***More data in one table space:*** A table space can hold 1 terabyte (TB) of data, instead of only 64 gigabytes (GB).
>
> ***More and larger partitions:*** Large table spaces can have a maximum of 254 partitions of 4 GB each, instead of only 64 partitions of 1 GB each.

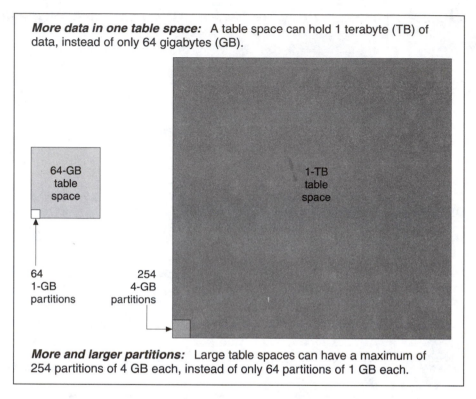

More data in one table space: A table space can hold 1 terabyte (TB) of data, instead of only 64 gigabytes (GB).

64-GB
table
space

1-TB
table
space

64
1-GB
partitions

254
4-GB
partitions

More and larger partitions: Large table spaces can have a maximum of 254 partitions of 4 GB each, instead of only 64 partitions of 1 GB each.

The original passage, from a software marketing brochure, accurately describes a product improvement. The words compare some very large numbers to some even larger numbers, but in text alone the words don't mean much, and their significance can easily be missed.

In the revised passage, simple but accurately scaled boxes dramatically compare the capacities in the new release with those in the previous release. Adding this illustration brings the meaning of the words to life.

Avoid illustrating what is already visible

It is a great temptation to illustrate, in online help or in printed information for a product with a graphical interface, the windows your text describes. Such illustrations can add visual interest to what might otherwise seem visually uninteresting. There are, however, several good reasons to avoid using images of windows:

❏ Most importantly, if the product's interface is well designed, you should not need to show a copy of it to explain how to use it! Indeed, the best interfaces are ones you need not explain at all.

❏ It is often difficult to ensure that the window image in your information reflects the current level of the product, and matches the window the user will see. An inaccurate image will confuse rather than help the user.

❏ If the product and the information will be translated, the window image will need to be recaptured from the translated product window. Translators might not have that capability. And even if they do, it will increase the cost of translation and the time needed for translation and testing.

❏ If users can see the window in the product, why reproduce it? If they must compare the window image with the actual window, their attention is divided.

❏ Adding window images increases page count, computer memory and storage usage, and overall cost.

If you *do* decide to use product windows as illustrations, follow these guidelines:

❏ Ensure that showing the windows actually adds to the user's understanding of the material; otherwise you are wasting space and diverting the user's focus.

❏ Capture all the windows or window fragments at the same scale, whenever possible, so that the text and graphical elements within them display at a consistent size.

❏ Show only the portions of the interface on which the user must focus to perform a task or to locate critical information, as in the following tutorial passage.

Original

To edit an existing document:

1. Click on **File** in the menu bar to open the **File** menu, as shown below.

2. Click on **Open** in the **File** menu.

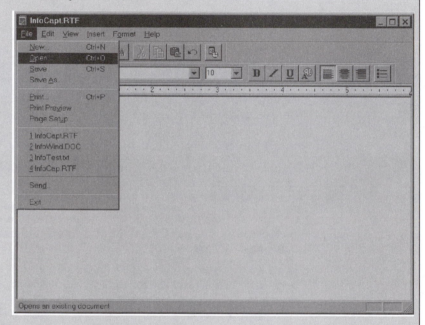

3. In the **Open** dialog box, select the drive and directory where the file is stored.

Revision

To edit an existing document:

1. Click on **File** in the menu bar to open the **File** menu.

2. Click on **Open** in the **File** menu.

3. In the **Open** dialog box, select the drive and directory where the file is stored.

The original example shows the entire window of the editing program, with the **File** menu dropped down and the **Open** action selected. This takes up a lot of space to show exactly what the user should be seeing on the monitor. Depending on how the user got to this point, however, the window on the monitor might appear somewhat different from the illustration. For the **Open** task, these differences are probably not important; what is important is selecting **Open** from the **File** menu.

The revised example shows only the **File** selection on the menu bar and the part of the menu that includes the selected **Open** action. This helps the user recognize where **Open** is in the menu, but does not include extra information that might distract the user or cause confusion because it isn't identical to the window displayed on the monitor.

Choose illustrations that complement the text

Use illustrations that help to complete and clarify the information. Relate illustrations to what the user wants to know.

Some users are word-oriented; others are picture-oriented. Showing as well as telling is an important way to ensure that both types of users get the point. You can show what is unwieldy to tell, highlight what is especially important, and provide clear symbols that users can remember.

Avoid duplicating information in an illustration; rather, use the illustration to expand on the text or to replace it. If the information lends itself to graphical depiction, minimize the written text and use the illustration to convey the information. At the same time, ensure that illustrations are neither too elementary nor too complex for the user. Illustrate the information that is most important for users to know, and show it as clearly as possible.

Consider how the illustrations in the following pair of passages work with the text.

Original

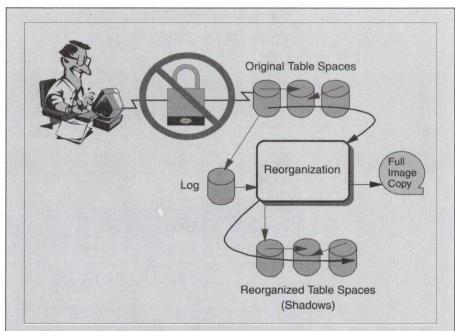

Original Table Spaces

Reorganization

Log

Full Image Copy

Reorganized Table Spaces (Shadows)

This figure represents what takes place during online reorganization. A shadow copy is made of the data sets. The log is applied to the shadow copy incrementally. When InfoBase is ready to apply the last increment, writers are drained. After applying the log, readers are drained and all users are switched to the new copy.

Both data and indexes are reorganized at the same time.

Revision

Previous releases of InfoBase require you to take your table spaces offline to reorganize them. A new option of the REORGANIZE utility allows you full read and write access to your data during most phases of reorganization.

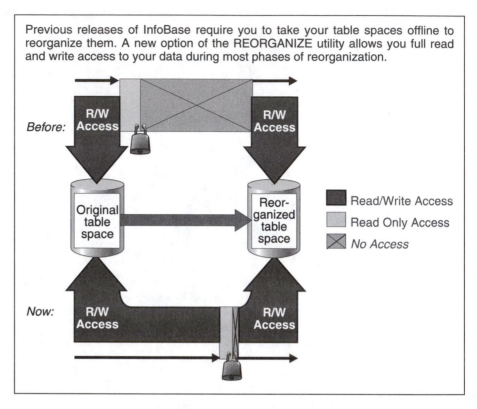

In the original illustration several arrows are used to indicate movement of data during the reorganization of an InfoBase table space, but the illustration doesn't explain what the arrows mean or how they differ. A cartoon figure of a user is included; it adds some levity and interest but no meaning, and is therefore just a distraction. The text that accompanies the illustration describes the program function without explaining how the figure illustrates it. We are left with an illustration that adds little to our understanding of the function.

The revised illustration, designed for a high-level, marketing-oriented book, shows what is significant about the new function to the user. The user wants to know why the reorganization function is better in the new release than in the previous release of the product. The illustration shows a comparison of the old function and the new, emphasizing the difference in read-write access availability during the reorganization process. Little or no text is needed to tell the user that the new function is an improvement over the old.

Present textual elements in a legible size and font

Choose a text type size that is appropriate for the particular combination of user, information type, and presentation medium to be used. A type size usually considered both economical and comfortable for adults to read in large blocks of print is 10 points. You can present some categories of information in smaller sizes if the user doesn't need to read large blocks of it at a time.

For online information, text should appear the equivalent of 10 or 12 point, or no less than 1/8 inch high. Most programs for delivery of information online are designed to display text at a readable size regardless of display resolution, but you should test your information at all supported display resolutions to verify its legibility.

Remember that if users will be viewing either printed or online information from farther away than about two feet, type size must be increased to retain legibility. If your information is being presented in a multimedia demonstration at a trade show, for example, where users stand about six feet away from the display monitor, text should be displayed at about 32 points to be legible.

The following table shows the point sizes that are appropriate for various types of information.

Minimum recommended type sizes		
Point size	Information type	Description
10*	Conceptual, guidance	Read from start to finish or at least in large, continuous blocks
9*	Reference	Read in limited blocks, usually a page or less, when looking for a small and specific subset of information
8*,†	Tables, illustrations, examples, syntax diagrams	In the context of a document element, read as small blocks of text: usually single sentences, short phrases, keywords, or lines of code.

Notes:

*When space is not restricted, or when the primary audience is over 40 years old, use larger type for continuous text.

†If the same information is to be presented in both printed and online formats, do not use smaller than 8 point type; if possible, use 9 point. Smaller type sizes, when displayed on many monitors, tend to break up or become so distorted as to be unreadable.

As important as choosing a legible type size is using a simple, clean, well-proportioned typeface, especially for online information. It is widely agreed that the serifs on the main strokes of characters in many typefaces help to lead the eye horizontally from one character to the next and thus facilitate the reading of continuous lines of text. The serifs on many typefaces, however, are very fine and can disappear from text displayed on most computer screens. For online information, therefore, select either of the following:

- ❏ A clean, uniform, sans-serif typeface such as Helvetica
- ❏ A typface with a strong, horizontal square or slab serif, such as Rockwell or Memphis

It's important to use legible type in artwork, as shown in the following pair of illustrations.

Original

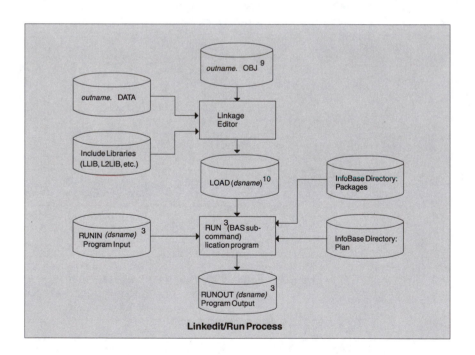

Linkedit/Run Process

Revision

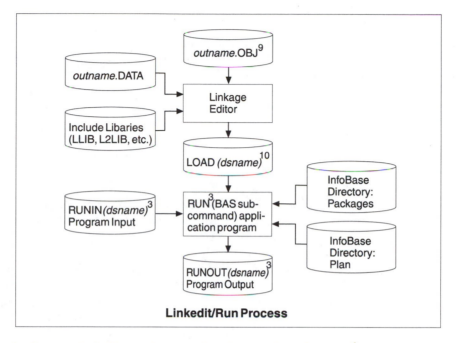

Linkedit/Run Process

In the original illustration, text has been reduced to 6 points to fit a lot of information into a small space. As a result, many users will struggle to read it.

In the revised illustration, by slightly enlarging the objects to accommodate larger text, the same illustration has been made much more legible without greatly increasing its overall size.

Use visual elements for emphasis

Visually emphasize the most important information. Graphical elements can help make the information's organization more obvious; they can also help to focus the user's attention on the most important information.

Consider, for example, how the relative size and weight of headings communicate their position in the organizational hierarchy. Highlighting a word or phrase gives it greater importance by making it stand out visually. You can extend this effect with graphical elements; symbols and icons, rules, tabs, and color can be powerful organizers.

If a phrase or paragraph is especially important, highlight it with a color or font change, or set it off from the rest of the text with a box or other structure. In an illustration, if one object or portion of the illustration is particularly significant, emphasize it with a slightly heavier outline, shading or color, or highlighted label. If necessary, try different techniques and then conduct an informal usability test to see which method best highlights the most important information. Sometimes, for example, adding shading to an object makes it recede rather than stand out; adding shading to the background and leaving the object unfilled is what emphasizes it.

Whatever methods you choose, use them consistently for similar emphasis throughout the information.

The following illustration is intended to show how an improvement to a product function enables users to merge information from two different tables in several different ways. Consider how shading might be used to make the illustration more effective.

Original

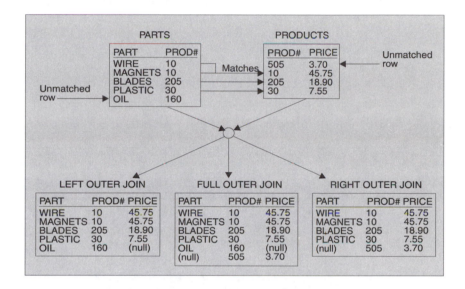

Revision

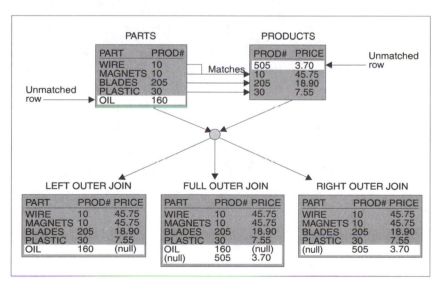

With the original illustration, users must read the entire contents of each box to perceive the relationships between them and thereby understand the meaning of the illustration. When shading is added to parts of the boxes, as shown in the revised illustration, the unshaded parts are emphasized, making it easier for users to identify the significant lines in each box and thus the relationships between them. Users can more easily grasp the point of the illustration.

Do not make your graphical elements so strong that they become the primary focus on the window or page. It's the information that's important; the structures that make it easier to find and understand should recede so that they simply support, but do not overpower, the information.

Compare the use of rules in the following two tables.

Original

Breed	Origin	Characteristics	Mane and tail type
Quarter horse	Breed developed in Western U.S.	Sprint speed; tight turns	Medium texture and thickness;mane often pulled or trimmed short
Morgan	Breed developed in Eastern U.S.	Versatility; endurance; driving; elegant trot	Thick, long, coarse
Arabian	Ancient breed developed in Arabian desert	Endurance; racing; elegance and flash	Fine and flowing; mane generally kept long
Appaloosa	Technically not a breed; rather, a set of coloring characteristics occurring in several breeds	Distinctive coloration	Medium coarse; usually sparse

Revision

Breed	Origin	Characteristics	Mane and tail type
Quarter horse	Breed developed in Western U.S.	Sprint speed; tight turns	Medium texture and thickness;mane often pulled or trimmed short
Morgan	Breed developed in Eastern U.S.	Versatility; endurance; driving; elegant trot	Thick, long, coarse
Arabian	Ancient breed developed in Arabian desert	Endurance; racing; elegance and flash	Fine and flowing; mane generally kept long
Appaloosa	Technically not a breed; rather, a set of coloring characteristics occurring in several breeds	Distinctive coloration	Medium coarse; usually sparse

The original table is easy to find on the page, but the information within it is overpowered by the table rules, which make it more difficult for the eyes to travel smoothly across the rows and from one row to the next. The revised table makes the organization of the information clear without imposing the rules as a barrier to the information flow. Faint rules separate rows, and consistently placed white space separates the columns, making their layout clear while allowing users to focus on the data.

Use visual elements logically and consistently

Choose a visual system to use throughout your information. If the style guidelines you are following (as discussed in "Follow style guidelines" on page 129), do not address consistent treatment of visual elements, work with a designer to establish a visual system. Then add the standards to your style guidelines, and stick to them! You should have guidelines that apply to headings, highlighting, font usage, example and syntax formats, list, table, and figure formats, indention, and graphic placements. If the same visual system is used throughout the information, users quickly learn where and how to find the information they need.

Attentive users notice even the smallest change in a visual system and assume it has significance. If it doesn't, or if you haven't explained the difference, they will be distracted and confused. Consider the significance of the placement of examples in the following passage.

Original

1. Decide which module to place in maintenance mode.
2. Stop all modules by entering the following command for each module in the group:

   ```
   -IN1G STOP INFOB MODE(QUIESCE)
   ```
3. Start the surviving member in maintenance mode by using the following command:

   ```
   -IN1G START INFOB ACCESS(MAINT)
   ```
4. Stop the surviving member by using the following command:

   ```
     -IN1G STOP INFOB MODE(QUIESCE)
   ```
5. Stop any IQMs that have not stopped, using the following command:

   ```
   STOP iqmproc
   ```

Revision

1. Decide which module to place in maintenance mode.

2. Stop all modules by entering the following command for each module in the group:

```
-IN1G STOP INFOB MODE(QUIESCE)
```

3. Start the surviving member in maintenance mode by using the following command:

```
-IN1G START INFOB ACCESS(MAINT)
```

4. Stop the surviving member by using the following command:

```
-IN1G STOP INFOB MODE(QUIESCE)
```

5. Stop any IQMs that have not stopped, using the following command:

```
STOP iqmproc
```

When some code examples are indented and others are not, as in the original passage, or are indented a different number of spaces, the user assumes the spacing is significant, and might as a result code an application incorrectly. In the revised example, code examples are aligned with the left margin of the list text. Users can be confident that code like the example need not be indented to work correctly.

Similarly, if every table has a different format, users must learn how to identify and read each table they encounter.

Visual Effectiveness

The following two tables, for example, both present information about a product, but in different formats.

Original

Table 1. Values Inserted in the INFODA

Value	Field	Description
INFODA	INFODAID	An "eye-catcher"
8816	INFODABC	The size of the INFODA in bytes ($16 + 44 \times 200$)
200	INFON	The number of occurrences of INFOVAR, set by the program
200	INFOD	The number of occurrences of INFOVAR actually used by the DESCRIBE statement
452	INFOTYPE	The value of INFOTYPE in the first occurrence of INFOVAR. It indicates that the first column contains fixed-length character strings, and does not allow null values.

INFO Data Type	InfoBasic Equivalent	Notes
SMALLINT	INTEGER*2	
INTEGER	INTEGER*4	
DECIMAL(p,s) or NUMERIC(p,s)	no exact equivalent	Use REAL*8
FLOAT(n) single precision	REAL*4	$1 \leq n \leq 21$
FLOAT(n) double precision	REAL*8	$22 \leq n \leq 53$
CHAR(n)	CHARACTER*n	$1 \leq n \leq 254$

Table 2. INFO Data Types Mapped to Typical InfoBasic Declarations

Revision

Table 1. Values Inserted in the INFODA

Value	Field	Description
INFODA	INFODAID	An "eye-catcher"
8816	INFODABC	The size of the INFODA in bytes ($16 + 44 \times 200$)
200	INFON	The number of occurrences of INFOVAR, set by the program
200	INFOD	The number of occurrences of INFOVAR actually used by the DESCRIBE statement
452	INFOTYPE	The value of INFOTYPE in the first occurrence of INFOVAR. It indicates that the first column contains fixed-length character strings, and does not allow null values.

Table 2. INFO Data Types Mapped to Typical InfoBasic Declarations

INFO Data Type	InfoBasic Equivalent	Notes
SMALLINT	INTEGER*2	
INTEGER	INTEGER*4	
DECIMAL(p,s) or NUMERIC(p,s)	no exact equivalent	Use REAL*8
FLOAT(n) single precision	REAL*4	$1 \leq n \leq 21$
FLOAT(n) double precision	REAL*8	$22 \leq n \leq 53$
CHAR(n)	CHARACTER*n	$1 \leq n \leq 254$

Before users can extract the important information from the second table in the original passage, they must identify how the table differs from the earlier one and then determine whether the differences have meaning. The inconsistent table format has slowed their progress and comprehension needlessly.

If table structures are consistent, as in the revised passage, users quickly learn to use the structure only as a guide and to focus on the information it contains.

Similar consistency guidelines apply to the design of multimedia presentations, demonstrations, and tutorials. Most multimedia development software offers an almost unlimited selection of window backgrounds, transitional effects, and ability to integrate audio and video clips. It is exciting to try all the different options, but *please* resist the urge to use all the graphic gimmicks at your disposal. Instead:

❏ Select a screen background that complements your presentation but doesn't overpower it, and use the same background throughout the presentation.

❏ If your presentation uses dynamic transitional effects such as "fades," choose one or two types and use them repeatedly. Remember that it is your information you want users to remember, not the power and versatility of the tool you used.

❏ Use consistent navigation methods and button placements throughout the presentation. This way, when the users see how the information is presented and learn how to navigate, they do not need to learn a different system on each new window and can concentrate on the information being presented.

What would users think if they tried to use the following pair of windows from the same presentation?

Original

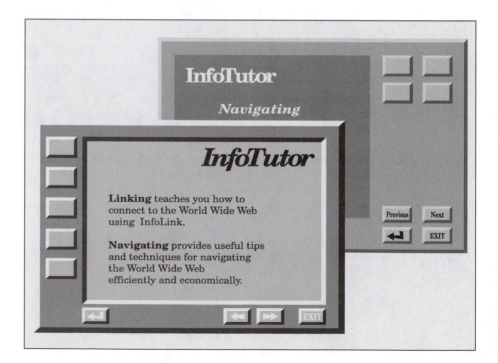

Revision

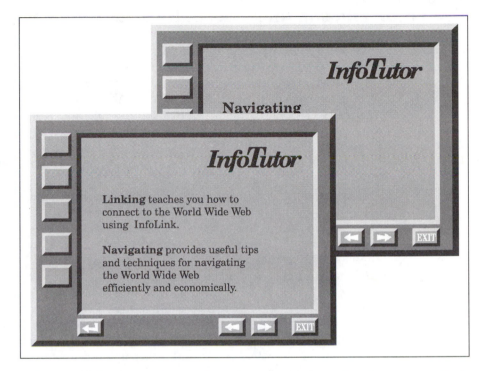

When using the original pair of windows, users must first determine which parts of each window contain significant information and then locate and understand how to move from that window to another one.

When the presentation methods are consistent, as in the revised example, users learn quickly the location of the visual elements in the window. Users then notice these elements only as enhancements to the information and can focus on the information rather than on the presentation methods and effects.

Use color and shading discreetly and significantly

Color can be very helpful in establishing a hierarchy of importance, providing visual breaks, and clarifying information. Information that is to be presented online can usually include multiple colors with little impact to cost. Color can be expensive to use in printed information, so you might need to restrict your color use. Even in black-and-white documents, though, shading can be just as effective in adding clarity and interest to your information.

As with all graphic techniques, color should be used to make the information easier to find, understand, and use; it should not so overpower the information presentation that it distracts or confuses the user.

Cool colors (blues and greens) recede, whereas warm colors (reds and oranges) advance. By placing cool and warm colors strategically, you can enhance the relative importance of information. Use bright red, however, only for warning and danger information.

Consider, too, the possible international use of your information. Some colors have different significance from culture to culture. Red, for example, signals danger in most Western cultures, but in Asia it represents happiness and is often worn by brides, and white is worn for mourning. If you are using color to convey meaning, check with international experts to ensure that you are not using it in an ambiguous or potentially offensive way.

Many colors appear only as shades of grey to some color-blind people, so your visual system should be able to stand on its own merit even if viewed in black and white. If you must use only one color (usually, but not always, black) you can use shading (tints, or screens, of black or the color) to help focus the user's attention on the most important information.

The following series of bar charts shows how shading can be used to enhance the information being conveyed.

Original

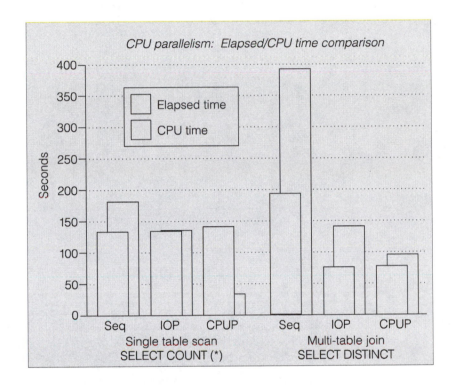

First Revision

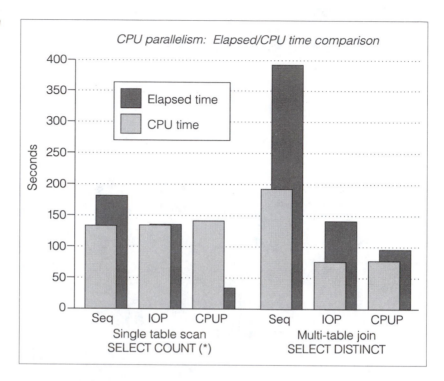

CPU parallelism: Elapsed/CPU time comparison

The original chart, with no color or shading, is almost meaningless because it's impossible to distinguish one set of bars from the other. Shading has been added to the revised chart to differentiate the bars for elapsed time from the bars for CPU time. The placement and shading of the two sets of bars could have any of several implications:

❏ Elapsed time is more important because its bars are darker
❏ CPU time is more important because its bars are in front
❏ Neither statistic is more important than the other.

The combination of shading and bar position in the first revised chart does not clearly emphasize one set of statistics over the other. If this is the message you want to convey, the design works as intended. If, however, you want to emphasize one set of statistics, a different design would make a stronger statement.

Second Revision

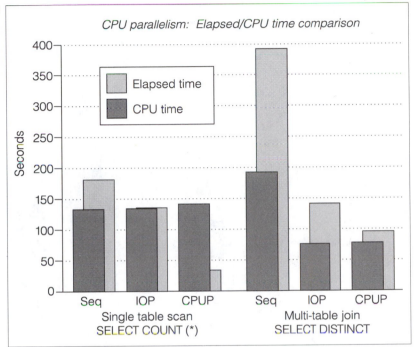

CPU parallelism: Elapsed/CPU time comparison

Third Revision

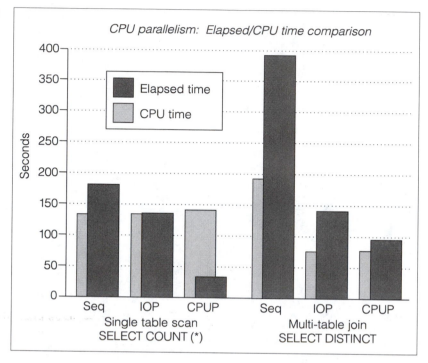

The darker, stronger shading in the second revised chart is on the set of bars in front; this shading clearly emphasizes CPU time. The third revised chart, however, emphasizes elapsed time not only by using the darker shading for its bars, but also by moving its bars to the front. Color (shading) has been combined with position to strengthen the message.

When selecting color and shading, consider the context within which your information will be viewed. If, for example, your information will be made available on the World Wide Web and will have links to other information, use the same color coding for links that is used in associated Web documents, or provide an obvious key that explains the color scheme you use. Also, test your information and its colors in as many as possible of the environments where it will be viewed. Differences in monitor specifications, resolutions, color modes and calibrations, Web browsers, operating environments, and room lighting can all affect how colors display and are perceived. You must ensure that the color scheme you've established has the effect you've intended.

Use visual cues to help users find what they need

Graphical elements, systematically and consistently used, can help users find information quickly.

In printed information, tabs or bleed bars (strips of color along the edge of a page) provide an easy way to help users find the beginning of a chapter or section. When users thumb through the book, the changing position of the tabs at the edge of the page tells them when they reach a new section.

Online interfaces often use icons to represent program and data objects. Well-designed icons can be easier to find than the names they represent, and can provide a lot of information about the characteristics of the objects they represent and their relationships to other objects. Iconic images are also used on buttons to represent program tools or the actions those tools perform.

You can use icons in both online and printed information to show users what information is where. This technique can be particularly helpful when most of the information is common to several environments, scenarios, or user subgroups, but some of the information applies to only a subset of the larger group.

Rather than repeating the common information for each subset, you can use a system of small graphics or icons, one for each unique situation, placed at the beginning of the subset information. This system helps users find information that pertains to them, as shown in the following pair of passages.

Original

To install InfoManager:

1. Place the CD in your computer's CD-ROM drive.

2. If installing in OS/2:

    a. Open an OS/2 window
    b. Change to the drive letter of your CD-ROM drive
    c. Type SETUPOS2.

    If installing in DOS:

    d. Boot DOS
    e. Change to the drive letter of your CD-ROM drive
    f. Type SETUPDOS

    If installing in Windows 95:

    g. Click on the **Start** button
    h. Select **Run** ...
    i. Type d:\SETUPW95 where d is the drive letter of your CD-ROM drive
    j. Click on the **OK** button.

3. Follow the instructions in the setup program for your environment.

Revision

> To install InfoManager:
>
> 1. Place the CD in your computer's CD-ROM drive.
>
> 2. Next:
>
> If installing in OS/2:
>
> > a. Open an OS/2 window
> > b. Change to the drive letter of your CD-ROM drive
> > c. Type SETUPOS2.
>
> If installing in DOS:
>
> > a. Boot DOS
> > b. Change to the drive letter of your CD-ROM drive
> > c. Type SETUPDOS
>
> If installing in Windows 95:
>
> > a. Click on the **Start** button
> > b. Select **Run** ...
> > c. Type d:\SETUPW95 where d is the drive letter of your CD-ROM drive
> > d. Click on the **OK** button.
>
> 3. Follow the instructions in the setup program for your environment.

In the original example, users must read all of the text to find the information that applies to the operating system that interests them. In the revised example, users need only look for the symbols that represent:

❏ Information specific to their operating system
❏ Common information.

Users can skip the sections that apply to other operating systems. Thus they can move more efficiently through the information without taking time to read the information that doesn't pertain to them.

Make your users' paths obvious. Ensure that they always know where to go next. This can be as simple as numbering the steps in a procedure or, in online information, highlighting links clearly and unambiguously.

Ensure that the retrievability aids you add are useful to as many of your users as possible, as in the following pair of passages.

Original

> With InfoBrowser you can:
>
> ☐ See a set of windows in one module
> ☐ See a single window
> ☐ Search a window or window set for a word
> ☐ Search a window or window set for a window element
> ☐ Run the SpellChecker

Revision

> With InfoBrowser you can:
>
> ☐ See a **set** of windows in one module
> ☐ See a **single window**
> ☐ **Search** a window or window set for a word
> ☐ Search a window or window set for a **window element**
> ☐ Run the **SpellChecker**

The original example shows an online help window on which the hypertext links are coded in a different color than the rest of the text. This difference makes the links obvious when viewed in color. But what if the window is displayed on a monochrome monitor or if the user is color-blind and cannot distinguish the color difference?

The revised example shows the same links both in a different color and underlined. Addition of the second visual cue enables color-blind users and users of monochrome displays to distinguish such links from normal text.

You might be required to integrate your information into an environment where a different visual system is used. If your information is to be placed on the World Wide Web, for example, you might need to provide links to Web pages that represent links with different colors or highlighting. If you are faced with such a situation, choose the visual system that is either the most prevalent or the most obvious and usable. If you're lucky, they'll be the same!

In sum

Use the guidelines in this chapter to ensure that technical information is visually effective. Refer to the examples in the chapter for practical applications of these guidelines.

When you review technical information for visual effectiveness, you can use this checklist in two ways:

❑ As a reminder of what to look for, to ensure a thorough review
❑ As an evaluation tool, to determine the quality of the information

You can apply the quality rating in the third column of the checklist to the guideline as a whole. Judging by the number and severity of items you found, decide how the information rates on each guideline for this quality characteristic. You can then add your findings to "Quality Checklist" on page 269, which covers all the quality characteristics.

Although the guidelines are intended to cover all areas for this quality characteristic, you might find additional items to add to the list for a guideline.

Guidelines for visual effectiveness	Items to look for	Quality rating
Balance the amount and placement of visual elements.	• Text is broken up by white space or varied structures. • White space appears intentional, not accidental.	1 2 3 4 5
Use graphics that are meaningful and appropriate.	• Graphics make the text more meaningful. • Graphics show only what the user needs to see.	1 2 3 4 5
Choose illustrations that complement the text.	• Illustrations provide significant information that the user needs. • Illustrations are not redundant with the text.	1 2 3 4 5
Present textual elements in a legible size and font.	• Sequential text is in a legible typeface and size. • Text is legible in less dense structures that use smaller text. • Typeface and size is appropriate for delivery medium and reading distance.	1 2 3 4 5
Use visual elements for emphasis.	• Visual elements emphasize important information. • Visual elements do not overpower the information.	1 2 3 4 5
Use visual elements logically and consistently	• Visual elements are presented and positioned consistently. • Navigational controls are supplied and positioned logically and consistently.	1 2 3 4 5
Use color and shading discreetly and significantly.	• Color or shading emphasizes the appropriate information. • Color and shading are used consistently. • Color does not convey meaning that might be ambiguous or offensive in another culture.	1 2 3 4 5
Use visual cues to guide users through their tasks.	• Visual elements help guide users to correct paths. • Visual cues are unambiguous.	1 2 3 4 5

Note: The scale for the quality rating goes from very satisfied (1) to very dissatisfied (5).

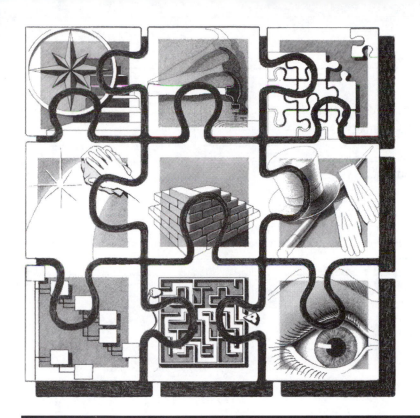

Part 4

Putting It All Together

Developing quality technical information involves all the quality characteristics. In this part we look at the interplay of characteristics. We also look at the roles of other people besides writers in the development cycle—technical reviewers and testers, human factors engineers, graphic designers, and editors.

Chapter 11

Applying More Than One Quality Characteristic

To explain each quality characteristic, we have treated each one separately. However, realistically, the characteristics work together. In fact, the characteristics often overlap, and it's hard to make clear boundaries between them.

A good index, for example, must be accurate, complete, well organized, clear, and stylistically consistent. A good index contributes primarily to retrievability but also to completeness and maybe task orientation (by including tasks as index entries). These are just some of the ways that the quality characteristics blend.

You can best improve a piece of writing by applying the guidelines for more than one quality characteristic.

Applying quality characteristics to guidance information

Let's consider some task help and how to improve it.

Original

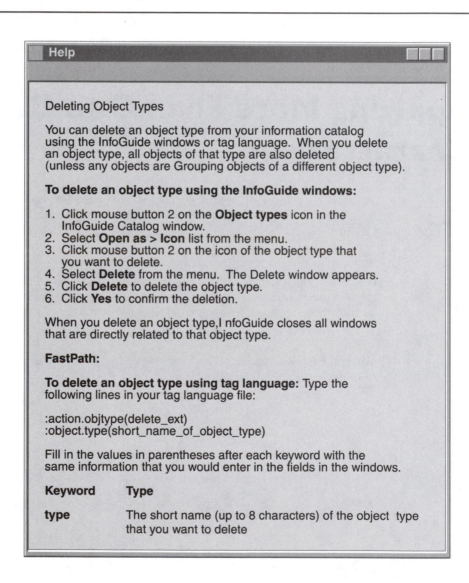

Help

Deleting Object Types

You can delete an object type from your information catalog using the InfoGuide windows or tag language. When you delete an object type, all objects of that type are also deleted (unless any objects are Grouping objects of a different object type).

To delete an object type using the InfoGuide windows:

1. Click mouse button 2 on the **Object types** icon in the InfoGuide Catalog window.
2. Select **Open as > Icon** list from the menu.
3. Click mouse button 2 on the icon of the object type that you want to delete.
4. Select **Delete** from the menu. The Delete window appears.
5. Click **Delete** to delete the object type.
6. Click **Yes** to confirm the deletion.

When you delete an object type, I nfoGuide closes all windows that are directly related to that object type.

FastPath:

To delete an object type using tag language: Type the following lines in your tag language file:

:action.objtype(delete_ext)
:object.type(short_name_of_object_type)

Fill in the values in parentheses after each keyword with the same information that you would enter in the fields in the windows.

Keyword	Type
type	The short name (up to 8 characters) of the object type that you want to delete

This help information is too long. Users must scroll to get all of the information to complete the task and, unless they scroll, will not know that the tag-language procedure is included. The problem is too much information, largely because of using one help window for both the primary audience for the information (users of the interface) and the secondary audience (users of the tag language).

You might also think of this as an organization or retrievability problem—not breaking down the information into chunks that are small enough for easy viewing. This arrangement also affects the task orientation of the information by using the same help window for two distinct sets of information for different audiences.

First Revision

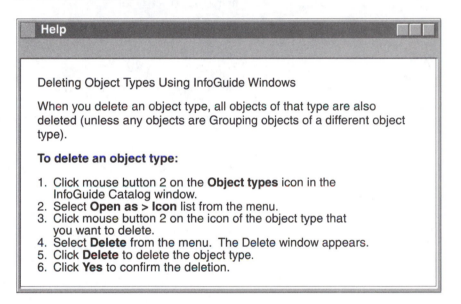

Help

Deleting Object Types Using InfoGuide Windows

When you delete an object type, all objects of that type are also deleted (unless any objects are Grouping objects of a different object type).

To delete an object type:

1. Click mouse button 2 on the **Object types** icon in the InfoGuide Catalog window.
2. Select **Open as > Icon** list from the menu.
3. Click mouse button 2 on the icon of the object type that you want to delete.
4. Select **Delete** from the menu. The Delete window appears.
5. Click **Delete** to delete the object type.
6. Click **Yes** to confirm the deletion.

Help

Deleting Object Types Using the Tag Language

When you delete an object type, all objects of that type are also deleted (unless any objects are Grouping objects of a different object type).

To delete an object type: Type the following lines in your tag language file:

```
:action.objtype(delete_ext)
:object.type(short_name_of_object_type)
```

Fill in the values in parentheses after each keyword with the same information that you would enter in the fields in the windows.

Keyword	Type
type	The short name (up to 8 characters) of the object type that you want to delete

---

The revised help information is split. Each audience can choose which help to go to—the one for interface or the one for tag language. Neither audience needs to read information that it's not interested in.

Now we need to refine each help window, eliminating internal redundancies or ambiguities. There might be more information that we can delete, and there might be some that we need to add or change.

Second Revision

Help

Deleting Object Types Using InfoGuide Windows

When you delete an object type, InfoGuide deletes all
objects of that type except for Grouping objects that
contain objects of a different object type. For example, InFoGuide
would not automatically delete a Multidimensional Model object that
contains Dimension objects.

To delete an object type:

1. Click mouse button 2 on in the InfoGuide Catalog window.
   Select **Open as > Icon** list from the menu.
   The Object Types window opens.
2. Click mouse button 2 on the icon of the object type that you
   want to delete. Select **Delete** from the menu.
   The Delete window opens.
3. Click **Delete** to delete the object type.
   A confirmation message appears.
4. Click **Yes** to confirm the deletion.
   InfoGuide closes all windows that are directly related to
   that object type.

Related Information
   Grouping objects
   Object types

Help □□□

Deleting Object Types Using the Tag Language

When you delete an object type, InfoGuide deletes all objects of that type except for Grouping objects that contain objects of a different object type. For example, InFoGuide would not automatically delete a Multidimensional Model object that contains Dimension objects.

To delete an object type:

1. Determine the short name of the object tyle that you want to delete. You can find the short name in the description of the object type.
2. Enter the following lines in your tag language file, filling in the appropriate short name:
   ```
   :action.objtype(delete_ext)
   :object.type(short_name_of_object_type)
   ```
3. Run the file.

Related Information
  Grouping objects
  Object types
  Tag-language syntax

The second revision addresses problems of clarity, concreteness, completeness, task orientation, accuracy, visual effectiveness, and style:

❑ Clarity and concreteness

The significance of Grouping objects was unclear. This revision links to a definition of the term and also to related information about the concept and object types. It also adds an example to help explain the exception.

❑ Completeness and task orientation

The revision consistently states the results of what the user does in the interface (using a pattern for what to present in the help). It also replaces the reference information with steps that fit the task.

❑ Accuracy

The step about filling in the values referred to fields in the interface that the interface help on deleting object types doesn't describe. In fact, the task help for using the interface indicates that there's nothing to enter, just items to select. The revision eliminated this reference.

❑ Visual effectiveness

The revision uses a picture of the icon rather than the verbal description of it. You might also add a symbol at the beginning of the help, for either the product or the topic—and follow the convention on other help windows too.

❏ Style

The style guidelines for this product caused two changes:
— Using *open* rather than *appear* for the action of windows
— Combining the mouse button click step and the select step into one step, to encourage thinking of these as one action

Applying quality characteristics to reference information

Here's a passage about a process rather than about a procedure for users to follow.

Original

> A link is established for each function request to the help processor. Each link has its own "current" help. Help selection from one link does not affect the current help on another link. Any link may select any help; more than one link may select the same help.
>
> The default help, 0, is considered current for the link unless changed by request on that link. The default is used before any help is created or selected on the link, or if the link explicitly deletes its own current help.

This passage is hard to understand. Why? The initial hurdle seems to be the passive voice. Who does what and when is unclear.

First Revision

> The help processor creates a link for each request that requires processing. Each link connects to a help window. Connecting a link to a help window does not change the connection between any other link and help window. Any link can connect to any help window; more than one link can connect to the same help.
>
> Initially, a link connects to the default help. Processing can connect the link to a new help window, or delete the help window that the link connects to. If processing deletes the help, the help processor resets the link to connect to the default help.

The first revision uses an active style and clarifies when the help processor is responsible for an action. Each sentence is easier to understand, but overall the meaning in the passage is still hard to find. The passage is still basically two dull paragraphs. To make the meaning obvious, we need to apply some techniques from retrievability and visual effectiveness.

Second Revision

Process of Linking Help Windows

User Action	Help Processor Action
No action	Connects to the default help
Requests help	Creates a link to the appropriate help
Requests different help	Links to a new help window
Leaves help	Returns to the default help

Principles for Linking Help Windows

- ❏ Any link can connect to any help window.
- ❏ More than one link can connect to the same help window.
- ❏ Connecting a link to a help window does not change the connection between any other link and help window.

The second revision uses headings, a table, and a list to show at a glance what the information is and how the parts relate to each other. You might decide that the passage needs to define some terms (such as *link* and *default help*) if they are not defined in earlier information. Scenarios would also help make the passage easier to understand.

Applying quality characteristics to combined guidance and reference information

Let's look at a passage that deals with a combination of guidance and reference information. This passage has lists, but a list isn't necessarily the best substitute for a paragraph.

Original

> The keywords are:
>
> ❏ The component identification keyword
>
>   This is the first keyword in the string. A search of the database with this keyword alone would detect all reported problems for the product.
>
> ❏ The type-of-failure keyword. The second keyword specifies the type of failure that occurred. Its values can be:
>
>   — ABENDxxx
>   — ABENDUxxx
>   — DOC
>   — PERFM
>   — MSGx
>   — INCORROUT
>   — WAIT/LOOP
>
> ❏ Symptom keywords
>
>   These can follow the keywords above and supply additional details about the failure. You select these keywords as you proceed through the type-of-failure keyword procedure that applies to your problem.
>
>   The suggested approach is to add symptom keywords to the search argument gradually so that you receive all problem descriptions that might match your problem. You can AND or OR additional keywords in various combinations to the keyword string to reduce the number of hits.
>
> ❏ Dependency keywords
>
>   These are program- or device-dependent keywords that define the specific environment in which the problem occurred. When added to your set of keywords, they can help reduce the number of problem descriptions you need to examine. See Appendix B, "Dependency Keywords," on page 303 for a list.

The original passage highlights the keywords, but the rest of the information is hard to sort out. The brief descriptions of the keywords leave you wondering "So what?" Buried in some of the paragraphs is information about how to use a keyword. However, you must read carefully to find it and then reorient it to something for a person to do.

If you back away from this information to get a broader perspective on its purpose to a user, you might decide that it communicates the concept of a keyword string.

First Revision

A keyword string is a set of words that you use to describe a problem with the product.

Type of Keyword	Description or Value	Use This Type of Keyword to...
Component identification	A set of characters representing the product or an orderable feature of the product	Find all reported problems with the product or with an orderable feature
Type of failure	☐ ABENDxxx ☐ ABENDUxxx ☐ DOC ☐ PERFM ☐ MSGx ☐ INCORROUT ☐ WAIT/LOOP	Refine your search to just that type of failure for the product or orderable feature
Symptom	Details about the failure	Refine your search gradually (by combining the symptom keywords in various ways) so that you receive all problem descriptions that might match your problem
Dependency	Program- or device-dependent keywords that define the environment in which the problem occurred*	Help reduce the number of problem descriptions you need to examine

*See Appendix B, "Dependency Keywords," on page 303 for a list.

The first revised passage makes the meaning obvious by its structure. It also presents the information from the user's point of view rather than from the point of view of the product. The information in the revised passage not only *looks* easier to understand; it *is* easier to understand. The writer has improved the clarity, task orientation, retrievability, and visual effectiveness of the passage.

Perhaps less obvious is that the writer has also improved the completeness of the passage by filling in gaps in the pattern of information. The original passage did not describe the first keyword, other than to say that it comes

245

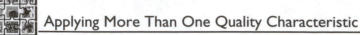

first—information that the table now conveys implicitly, through the order of the keywords from top to bottom. The original passage also did not give a use for the type-of-failure keyword. The table includes both of these items.

Second Revision

A keyword string is a set of descriptive words that you use to identify a problem with the product.

Type of Keyword	Description or Value	Use This Type of Keyword to...	Example of a Keyword String
Component identification	A set of characters representing the product or an orderable feature of the product	Find all reported problems with the product or with an orderable feature	CKJPROD
Type of failure	☐ ABENDxxx ☐ ABENDUxxx ☐ DOC ☐ PERFM ☐ MSGx ☐ INCORROUT ☐ WAIT/LOOP	Refine your search to just that type of failure for the product or orderable feature	CKJPROD WAIT
Symptom	Details about the failure	Refine your search gradually (combining the symptom keywords in various ways) so that you receive all problem descriptions that might match your problem	CKJPROD WAIT CYCLE
Dependency	Program- or device-dependent keywords that define the environment in which the problem occurred*	Help reduce the number of problem descriptions you need to examine	CKJPROD WAIT CYCLE AS4

*See Appendix B, "Dependency Keywords," on page 303 for a list.

The second revision adds a column for an example to the table. An example helps users see more easily what the rest of the information is about and relate the information to a keyword string of their own. The writer has made the passage more concrete.

Revising technical information

Your first approach with information that you're revising might be to consider whether the information is needed at all. Think about the guidelines for task orientation and completeness in particular. Maybe some information doesn't belong, as in the help example that offered two sets of instructions for two different audiences. Maybe a different viewpoint on the information is needed. For example, as with the keyword example, you might need to state the concept clearly and play up the task information so that users can quickly see the significance and usefulness of the reference information.

Maybe you need first to "translate" the information from technobabble into something more comprehensible. This translation is like the first revision in the example about links and help windows. After you understand the information, you can decide how best to present it.

The process of revising requires you to:

1. Understand.
2. Improve the information.
3. Improve the information some more.

You can use the quality characteristics to approach technical information systematically so that you can more easily write and revise it.

247

Chapter 12

Reviewing and Evaluating Technical Information

Reviewing and evaluating technical information can take several forms, depending on who the reviewer is.

Just as reviewers have special skills, they also have different areas of focus. Not every reviewer needs to look for all the same items. For example, programmers need not comment on style, because that is the domain of editors.

Every writer needs reviewers—other pairs of eyes to see the information afresh. Reviewers bring their own skills and perspectives to the information.

This chapter deals with reviews by these different kinds of reviewers: technical reviewers and testers, actual users or people similar to them, editors, and graphic designers.

Inspecting technical information

A technical reviewer is an expert in the subject covered by the technical information. In general, technical reviewers are best qualified to evaluate the accuracy and completeness of technical information.

The technical reviewer's role is to:

❏ Read the information critically, or use it, or both.
❏ Find problems with the information.
❏ Report the problems in a way that helps the writer understand the problems and fix them.

As a reviewer, put yourself in the place of the user as you read or use the information. Ask yourself:

"If I were the user, could I find, understand, and use this information?"

Do not assume that because you understand something, a user will also—unless your skills and situation are very like those of a typical user.

If you are reviewing online information, you probably need to look at the information online, not just in a printed form.

See "Who Checks Which Quality Characteristics?" on page 273 for a table that summarizes what technical reviewers should look for.

When you report problems, it's not much help to say just:

"I don't like it."
"It's wrong."
"This needs fixing."

Be specific about what's wrong and suggest a solution, as in:

"This paragraph goes into too much detail about the process. I doubt users need that much."
"All message identifiers have eight characters. Change to eight throughout."
"Aligning the columns in this code as I've shown would be what most users expect."

Even with problems of accuracy and completeness, there can be more than one fix. Give enough information that a writer can understand the reasoning and discern the best fix.

Applying the guidelines from the earlier chapters in this book can help you be specific about typical problems and suggest solutions.

Testing information for usability

One way you can improve and validate the quality of your information is to test it for usability. Through usability testing, you can find problems especially in task orientation, completeness, accuracy, clarity, and retrievability.

Techniques for testing information for usability range from formal studies to informal reviews. The tests described in Table 2 are done in a usability laboratory with actual users or with people whose experience and skills make them representative of users. You can test the information in the context of using the product.

Table 2. Usability tests in a usability laboratory

Type of Test	Procedure	Measurements	Goal
Formal test	Users perform scenario-based tests on the product and information. Test team observes users, records actions, later does statistical analysis on data.	Success on a task and amount of time to perform each task	Results that can be replicated and generalized to other situations
Informal test	Similar to a formal test but with fewer users and fewer scenarios to test. Tests are sometimes iterative (test, improve, retest, improve, retest, finalize).	Less formal	Results that apply to the specific situation

Formal tests are generally more difficult to design and take longer to conduct, although they yield more reliable results than other approaches. Formal testing may be appropriate if the impact of your test will be wide ranging. For example, if the information you are testing is to be used by several products, or if it will be a template for other information, you will want to have reliable results. In this case, it's probably worth the extra time, effort, and expense to do formal testing with a representative sample of users.

However, if the scope of the information is small or if the product your information supports is a tactical solution that will be replaced, one of the less formal techniques of usability testing is probably sufficient.

There are several possibilities for testing information outside a usability laboratory with actual users, perhaps during a beta program, as shown in Table 3.

Table 3. Usability tests with users outside a usability laboratory

Type of Test	Procedure	What Is Tested
Instrumented beta	Beta code includes "hooks," which make it possible to record which help windows users access and when. Programmers must provide the necessary hooks, and users must agree to this form of data collection.	Navigation and content of online help windows
User edits or reviews	Users review the information and offer recommendations for improvement. Often they are asked to rate the information quality on a scale, and their evaluation is tracked during the beta test.	Information about product in beta test
Field observation	Writers visit users and observe them using the product and information.	Product and information in a real-life situation
Survey or questionnaire	Users answer questions about the quality of the information and product.	Product and information

Using any of these forms of feedback, writers can change the information to fix problems and improve the quality. When writers are uncertain about a problem or how to fix it, they can return to the users to get more information or ask another set of users.

Some testing can be done internally, without real users. Tests involving people such as programmers, writers, and usability specialists can yield valuable information and yet not require a lot of time to prepare and run. In a walkthrough, the people who are involved in developing the information try to use the information in a realistic way, by performing procedures and following instructions. This type of testing also yields information that writers can use to fix problems.

Editing and evaluating technical information

Conventional editing results in comments about the weaknesses in information. In addition, you can use the quality characteristics to categorize the strengths and weaknesses. You might need to modify your approach to editing. This section describes how to edit guidance and reference information, both online and printed, and apply the quality characteristics to your editing, as shown in Table 4.

Table 4. How to Edit Guidance and Reference Information (Part 1 of 2)

What to Do	Guidance Information Online	Guidance Information Printed	Reference Information Online	Reference Information Printed
Prepare to edit				
☐ Learn about the plan for the information	✓	✓	✓	✓
☐ Check earlier edition, if there is one		✓		✓
☐ Make sure you have:				
— Online access to the product and information	✓	✓	✓	✓
— Complete copy of the online information	✓		✓	
Get an overview				
☐ Survey the information, especially visual elements	✓	✓	✓	✓
☐ Study the front matter, especially table of contents		✓		✓
☐ Access the information from the product; navigate through it briefly	✓		✓	
Read and edit the information				
☐ Edit as you read	✓	✓	✓	✓
☐ Check especially for:				
— Factual consistency	✓	✓	✓	✓
— Organizational consistency	✓	✓	✓	✓
— Appropriate level of detail	✓	✓	✓	✓
— Appropriate examples and visual elements	✓	✓	✓	✓
— Consistent style	✓	✓	✓	✓
☐ Make a list of the kinds of information			✓	✓

Table 4.   How to Edit Guidance and Reference Information (Part 2 of 2)

What to Do	Guidance Information		Reference Information	
	Online	Printed	Online	Printed
Look for information				
❑ Check access paths for items on your list.			✓	✓
❑ Search for terms that users will need	✓	✓	✓	✓
❑ Check that links lead to relevant information	✓		✓	
❑ Check that cross-references lead to relevant information		✓		✓
Summarize your findings	✓	✓	✓	✓
Confer with the writer	✓	✓	✓	✓

Prepare to edit

Familiarize yourself with the general plan for the information before you begin editing it. Among the useful things you should know before you begin are:

❑ Audience—job tasks, experience level

❑ Graphic design (including visual elements such as tabs and color)

❑ Medium (such as help, wizard, printed book)

❑ Codes for color and highlighting if you're editing only a printed form of online information

❑ Expected number of windows for online information

A list of windows that indicates the subordination of windows is helpful, but not necessary.

❑ Information about planned changes in content

❑ What style guidelines apply

For printed information that isn't new, browse the latest edition if you have time and access to the book. You will probably see more clearly how the new edition is meant to differ from its predecessor.

The purpose of all this preparation is to develop an idea of what the finished information is meant to contain and look like. This preparation gives you a helpful set of expectations, and enables you to see what has and hasn't been realized in the information.

Get an overview

When you begin editing information, survey it as a whole, as a user might.

Pay attention to the visual elements:

- ❏ Is the information presented in an attractive way?
- ❏ Is there a balance between text and graphical elements?
- ❏ Are tables and lists used effectively?
- ❏ Are the type styles helpful or distracting?

For guidance information

Focus on task orientation by asking:

- ❏ Is the intended audience clear?
- ❏ Does the table of contents clearly show the real tasks for the product?
- ❏ Are the tasks presented in a logical sequence?
- ❏ Do all necessary tasks appear to be included?
- ❏ Is task help accessible from the point where a user would need help?
- ❏ Can a user read the task help while doing the steps?
- ❏ What is the pattern of information for presenting tasks?
- ❏ Do task windows provide links to supporting reference information?

For printed guidance information, studying the table of contents and the preface or introduction can help you determine the task orientation and organization of the information as a whole. You can get an idea of how complete the information is by checking whether all necessary tasks are included and whether all required parts of the front and back matter are in place.

Checking the contents window for online guidance information should also give you an idea of the task orientation and completeness of the information.

For reference information

Focus on retrievability by asking:

- ❏ What retrievability aids does the information use? If online, does the information use color or graphics to draw the eye to topics that recur (like restrictions on use or platform-dependent information)? If printed, does the information use aids such as bleed tabs, in addition to the usual table of contents, index, and running feet or running heads?

- ❏ Does the organization enhance retrievability? Will the subdivisions of information in the table of contents seem logical to someone looking up information?

❑ Do the type style and format enhance retrievability? For example, do code examples stand out as examples? Is the explanation of a syntax element easy to pick out?

You can also consider the organization and completeness of reference information by asking:

❑ If the information explains commands or programming statements, are the explanations ordered alphabetically by command or statement name?

❑ If the information explains messages, are the explanations ordered numerically by message identifier?

❑ If the information contains syntax diagrams, does it also have an explanation of how to read the diagrams?

❑ Are the headings appropriate for reference information? (Gerund phrases would indicate that guidance information has been mistakenly included.)

Read and edit the information

Read and edit the information in detail. For printed information, this reading should be linear, from front to back. For online information, establish an order for selecting and reading the information. Save more active testing, searching, and using the information for the next step.

After you get into the material, you will probably want to make notes of items to add to the style guidelines and items to watch out for that you suspect might be a problem. At some point you can begin to list problems, perhaps under the quality characteristic where you think they apply.

For guidance information, keep these questions in mind:

❑ Can I understand the steps in a procedure?
❑ Do the procedures tell me what I need to know to do the job?
❑ Is the information easy to navigate online? Is the sequence clear?
❑ Can I understand parts the first time I read them?
❑ Are new terms defined?
❑ Do I see anything obviously inconsistent or incorrect?
❑ Are the transitions from topic to topic logical?

For reference information, keep in mind that users will not read it cover to cover, or even section by section. They will enter it almost anywhere, in search of small bits of information. So as you read and edit, make a list of the kinds of information you come across—syntax diagrams, keyword explanations, restrictions, platform considerations, examples, and so on. You will use this list in the next step when you check retrievability.

Use the checklists at the end of each chapter in this book to help ensure that you look for the problems related to each quality characteristic. If you find more problems, add them to the lists where appropriate. Here's a brief list of major areas to check: factual consistency, organizational consistency, appropriate level of detail, appropriate examples and visual elements, consistent style.

Check for factual consistency

Make sure that the information in tables and figures agrees with the surrounding text. Information on the same topic should be consistent.

Make sure the keyword relationships shown in syntax diagrams agree with the explanations of the keywords. For example, a diagram might show that keyword X and keyword Y can coexist in the same command, but the explanations of X and Y might suggest that they are incompatible. Either the diagram or the explanations need to be fixed.

Also look at the examples and ensure that they can actually be derived from the syntax. Make sure that the examples and supporting text agree and that scenarios are consistent.

Check for organizational consistency

Expect to find repeated headings in chapters or windows, especially those that describe commands or programming statements. This repetition is common for headings at lower levels. For example, an operator's reference might have these headings for every command: "Format," "Environments," "Keywords," "Usage," "Restrictions," and "Examples." Users would be confused if they found different headings under different commands, if some commands had all these headings and some had fewer, or if the sequence of headings varied from one command to another.

Even when a set of headings is used consistently, you should ensure that the same kind of information falls under a given heading, from one context to another. For example, the kind of information that falls under "Usage" in one context shouldn't appear under "Restrictions" in another.

Check for appropriate level of detail

The need for some details depends on the experience level of the audience. Some other details are needed by any users and must be consistently provided. As you read the explanations of interface elements (fields, buttons, commands, statements, keywords), for example, make sure the purpose they serve is clearly stated. A similar requirement holds for examples: the purpose or effect of examples must be clear.

Check for appropriate examples and visual elements

Looking at one type of element such as examples or tables can reveal problems you wouldn't otherwise notice. Examples and visual elements are very important to users and so merit special attention. Consider, for example, whether the content of tables and graphics effectively supports or replaces text.

Check for consistent style

Notice choices in matters of style, and make these choices consistent throughout the information. Examples of style choices to check are terminology; highlighting; presentation syntax diagrams; and parallelism of headings, list items, index entries, and examples.

Look for information

Check whether reference information has effective access paths to each of the kinds of information that you identified while reading the information. Give special attention to the index: every item on your list should be represented by many index entries.

For online information, check links or cross-references between helps to see whether information is linked appropriately. For printed guidance information, look in the table of contents or index for topics you have read; you should be able to find them again.

This search gives you an idea of how useful, accurate, and complete the retrievability devices are.

Summarize your findings

Use the checklist at the end of each chapter in this book to summarize the kinds of problems found.

If a graphic designer has also reviewed the information, combine the comments resulting from that review with your own before making your final assessment. See "Reviewing the visual elements" on page 262 for guidelines for reviewing the visual elements.

Your comments in the draft and the summary tell writers and planners about changes that will improve the quality of the information. Your summary should identify the weaknesses that in your opinion would have the most serious impact on how satisfied users are with the information.

Assigning problems to the quality characteristics

It's not always obvious how to classify a problem. Some problems, for example, affect more than one quality characteristic. In that case, consider the importance of the problem to the user. When a problem might affect any of two or more quality characteristics, give preference to the quality characteristic that is more important to the user. For example, a typo might be either a style problem or an accuracy problem, depending on how the typo affects the user. Transposing letters in a file name has a definite impact on accuracy, but *form* instead of *from* might hardly be noticed.

However, also note when a problem affects another quality characteristic. For example, note when a problem that you report in concreteness also has an effect on retrievability. This information helps the writer understand the extent of a problem's impact.

Style has a dependence on other quality characteristics, because some characteristics provide a basis for style decisions. For example, a style guideline might be made because following it promotes clarity, visual effectiveness, or retrievability. Style in itself does not have a rationale other than the force of convention.

You might choose to put a deviation from the chosen style guidelines in another quality characteristic when *both* of the following statements are true:

❑ Not following the style has a major impact on the other quality characteristic.

❑ The error occurs frequently. The writer seems to have forgotten the rationale or seems not to understand it.

You might find other "rules" for assigning problems to quality characteristics as you become more familiar with thinking about problems in terms of the quality characteristics and their effect on users.

Assigning quality ratings

After you categorize and summarize your comments, you can assign ratings to the quality characteristics. A quality rating is a numeric representation of the quality of information on a particular characteristic or overall. You can use this quality rating as an indicator of the progress of information either during its development cycle or from release to release.

The quality rating is the result of:

❑ Thoroughly editing the information
❑ Summarizing your editorial comments
❑ Rating each of the nine quality characteristics

You can use the "Quality Checklist" on page 269 to summarize your ratings. To say how satisfied you are with each quality characteristic, review the strengths and weaknesses you classified in a given quality characteristic and then consider the meanings of the scale points.

As you work with quality ratings, you will probably find situations where one problem could be enough to bring a quality characteristic down a point and where many small problems would not change a score. Again, you will probably derive some rules to help you decide what ratings to give. You might decide, for example, that when in doubt about a rating for a quality characteristic, pick the better rating.

However, assigning a quality rating is not like grading a math test, where one knocks off points for errors. Assigning a quality rating is more like comparing the information to what you consider average and then figuring out whether the problems that you found make the information better or worse than average.

You also need to take into account the stage of development that the information is at. For example, an early draft might not have all the information, but the writer should be able to indicate what is missing and where it will go; the effect on completeness would be less a problem than in a final draft.

Consider also your level of knowledge about the product in determining the quality rating of information on accuracy. You might consider feedback from technical reviewers on this quality characteristic.

Confer with the writer

Even though writers need reviewers (especially editors), few people have thick skins when their writing draws critical comments. It's best to meet with the writer to go over your comments and make sure that the person understands your suggested changes and your reasons for them. After all, you and the writer are working together to create the best possible information for your users.

Reviewing the visual elements

Graphic designers review information for how well the visual elements attract and motivate users and convey the intended meaning.

As you've seen in Chapter 10, there are many visual elements and many ways for them to go awry.

These are the steps for conducting a review of visual elements:

1. Prepare to review.
2. Get an overview.
3. Review individual graphic elements.
4. Summarize your findings.
5. Confer with the writer.

Prepare to review

Familiarize yourself with the plan for the information.

Get copies of information design specifications and style guidelines that the writer used. Thoroughly understand the parts that address visual design.

If you are performing your review in association with an edit, schedule your review to follow the edit. Get the draft with the editor's comments.

Before you begin your review, you should know:

❏ Type of information (such as guidance, reference, marketing)
❏ Delivery medium (such as online, Web, multimedia)
❏ Target audience, their tasks and experience level
❏ Visual design specifications and guidelines

Get an overview

Use the same draft (if printed material) that the editor used, but for your first pass through the information, disregard the editor's comments.

Step or page through the information, noting both positive and negative impacts of its presentation:

❏ Are pages visually balanced?

❏ Is white space used effectively?

❏ Are task lists obvious? Is their sequence clear?

❏ Is the information free of visual clutter? Note, for example:
— Irrelevant graphics
— Unnecessary lines and symbols
— Overabundant highlighting
— Distracting background patterns

❏ Is the typeface and size used for text in each element legible?

❏ Are elements presented consistently and according to style guidelines? Note, for example:
— Lists
— Tables
— Programming syntax
— Headings
— Highlighting

❏ Are all illustrations rendered in a consistent style? Note, for example:
— Line characteristics
— Color
— Shading
— Fill patterns
— Fonts

❏ Is color used to enliven and enhance the information, without overpowering or distracting the user?

❏ Is the information broken into manageable chunks?

❏ Are visual retrievability aids used effectively? Note, for example:
— Tabs
— Rules
— Captions
— Icons

❏ Is the organization of the information clear at a glance?

When reviewing online information, consider:

❏ Can visual elements be viewed in all supported resolutions? Are they usable in these resolutions?
❏ Are backgrounds simple and unobtrusive?
❏ Are links clearly identified?
❏ Are navigational aids consistent in design and placement?
❏ Are navigational aids obvious?

When reviewing multimedia presentations, consider:

❏ Are all windows laid out consistently?
❏ Is a consistent, clear color scheme used throughout?
❏ Do visual transitions all use the same one or two methods?

Review individual graphic elements

Go through the information again from the beginning, focusing on individual visual elements that you feel need attention.

If an edit was done, review the editor's comments on visual elements and design. Note whether you agree and, if you disagree, why. At places where the editor has suggested adding or changing a visual element, read the surrounding text and make recommendations, if possible, on the design of the visual element.

Consider these issues as you focus on individual elements:

❑ Are illustrations meaningful and appropriate?

❑ Is the artwork legible and clear in *all* presentation media and formats?

❑ In online information and interfaces:

— Are the icons unambiguous and meaningful?

— If you have seen these icons before, is their meaning here consistent with their earlier use?

— Are the images used for toolbar actions clear?

— Are common images used for common actions (for example, scissors for "cut")?

— Is the meaning of toolbar buttons intuitive? If not, are they supplemented with hover help?

❑ In animations or video clips:

— Are the animations smooth?

— If the animations are continuously looping, can they be stopped? Is it easy to figure out how to stop them?

— Can animations that run once and stop be run again? Is it easy to figure out how to rerun them?

Summarize your findings

Gather your significant concerns and comments into a report. Note the quality characteristic that you think is most seriously affected by each problem. The ultimate impact of a visual effectiveness problem is often to one of the other quality characteristics described in this book, such as clarity, accuracy, or organization.

If you have identified areas where you disagree with the editor, make note of these in your report, too.

As much as possible, recommend solutions to problems that you have identified. It helps to be familiar with the tools used to develop the information and its visual components. You can understand the capabilities and limitations of the tools.

Confer with the editor or writer

If you did your review as part of an edit, give your comments and summary to the editor to compile into a summary report.

Schedule a meeting with the writer or both the writer and the editor to discuss the results of your visual review. If a designer or illustrator was involved in developing the visual elements, include that person in the meeting, too. At the meeting, reach agreement among all participants on changes to visual elements.

Part 5

Appendixes, Bibliography, and Glossary

Appendix **A**

Quality Checklist

After you edit or review technical information, you can use the Quality Checklist to summarize your ratings for each quality characteristic. If you used the checklist at the end of each chapter to keep track of your findings, you can pull together your ratings here. You can then get an overall picture of the strengths and weaknesses of the information and make a plan for working on the weaknesses.

Table 5. Quality Checklist (Part 1 of 3)

Quality Characteristic and Guidelines	Quality Rating
Easy to Use	
Task Orientation (page 11)	1 2 3 4 5
Information is appropriate for the intended audience.	1 2 3 4 5
Information is presented from the user's point of view.	1 2 3 4 5
The focus is on real tasks.	1 2 3 4 5
A practical reason for information is evident.	1 2 3 4 5
Titles and headings reveal tasks.	1 2 3 4 5
Accuracy (page 29)	1 2 3 4 5
Information has been verified.	1 2 3 4 5
Corrections have been made based on findings from accuracy-checking tools	1 2 3 4 5
Information reflects the current product.	1 2 3 4 5
Information on a topic is consistent.	1 2 3 4 5
References to related information are correct.	1 2 3 4 5
Completeness (page 49)	1 2 3 4 5
All topics that support users' tasks are covered, and only those topics.	1 2 3 4 5
Each topic has just the detail users need.	1 2 3 4 5
Patterns of information ensure proper coverage.	1 2 3 4 5
Information is repeated only when needed.	1 2 3 4 5
Easy to Understand	
Clarity (page 75)	1 2 3 4 5
The focus is on the meaning.	1 2 3 4 5
Language is unambiguous.	1 2 3 4 5
The elements are short.	1 2 3 4 5
The elements flow from one to another.	1 2 3 4 5
Similar topics are presented in a similar way.	1 2 3 4 5
Technical terms are necessary and appropriate.	1 2 3 4 5
Each term that is new to the intended user is defined.	1 2 3 4 5
Concreteness (page 107)	1 2 3 4 5
Examples are appropriate for the audience and topic.	1 2 3 4 5
Examples are realistic, accurate, and up to date.	1 2 3 4 5
Examples are easy to find.	1 2 3 4 5
Scenarios illustrate tasks and provide product overviews.	1 2 3 4 5
Code examples are easy to adapt.	1 2 3 4 5
Unfamiliar information is related to familiar information.	1 2 3 4 5

Table 5. Quality Checklist (Part 2 of 3)

Quality Characteristic and Guidelines	Quality Rating
Style (page 125)	1 2 3 4 5
Grammar, spelling, and punctuation are correct.	1 2 3 4 5
Style guidelines are followed.	1 2 3 4 5
Style is active.	1 2 3 4 5
Instructions are in the imperative mood.	1 2 3 4 5
Tone is appropriate and consistent.	1 2 3 4 5
Easy to Find	
Organization (page 141)	1 2 3 4 5
Organization of guidance information is sequential.	1 2 3 4 5
Organization of reference information is logical.	1 2 3 4 5
Organization of information is consistent.	1 2 3 4 5
Help is organized into discrete topics and types.	1 2 3 4 5
Main points are emphasized; secondary points are subordinated.	1 2 3 4 5
Topics that are divided have at least two subtopics.	1 2 3 4 5
Branches are used only if helpful.	1 2 3 4 5
Users can see how the pieces fit together.	1 2 3 4 5
Retrievability (page 169)	1 2 3 4 5
Text is broken into manageable chunks.	1 2 3 4 5
The index has predictable entries.	1 2 3 4 5
The index is complete and correct.	1 2 3 4 5
Linked-to information is easy to find on the target window or page.	1 2 3 4 5
Introductory sections reveal the order of topics to come.	1 2 3 4 5
Table of contents has an appropriate level of detail.	1 2 3 4 5
Key terms are easy to find.	1 2 3 4 5
Visual Effectiveness (page 195)	1 2 3 4 5
The amount and placement of visual elements are balanced.	1 2 3 4 5
Graphics are meaningful and appropriate.	1 2 3 4 5
Illustrations complement the text.	1 2 3 4 5
Textual elements are in a legible size and font.	1 2 3 4 5
Visual elements are used for emphasis.	1 2 3 4 5
Visual elements are logical and consistent.	1 2 3 4 5
Color and shading are discreet and significant.	1 2 3 4 5
Visual cues help users find what they need.	1 2 3 4 5

Table 5.   Quality Checklist (Part 3 of 3)

Quality Characteristic and Guidelines	Quality Rating

Legend:

1—Very satisfied
Among the best; could be used as a model.

2—Satisfied
Solid, professional work.

3—Neither satisfied nor dissatisfied
OK—par for the course; overall, neither praiseworthy nor blameworthy.

4—Dissatisfied
Clearly subpar.

5—Very dissatisfied
Among the worst.

Who Checks Which Quality Characteristics?

Writers have responsiblity for checking all of the items that affect the quality of technical information. Technical editors have a similar responsiblity except that they are not responsible for verifying the accuracy of the information.

The more limited responsibility of technical reviewers (people skilled in the content of the information) spans several quality characteristics—primarily accuracy, completeness, concreteness, and visual effectiveness. Sometimes technical reviewers may be asked to check certain aspects of clarity and retrievability.

In addition to checking all aspects of visual effectiveness, graphic designers need to check certain aspects of clarity, concreteness, style, and retrievability.

Peer editors (or copyeditors in some situations) typically do their checking near the end of the development cycle. They need to check certain aspects of all the quality characteristics.

Table 6.   Who Checks Which Quality Characteristics (Part 1 of 3)

Quality Characteristic and Guidelines	Writers	Technical Reviewers	Technical Editors	Graphic Designers	Peer Editors
Easy to Use					
Task Orientation					
Information is appropriate for intended audience.	✓	✓	✓		
Information is presented from user's point of view.	✓		✓		
Focus is on real tasks.	✓		✓		
Practical reason for informaton is evident.	✓		✓		
Titles and headings reveal tasks.	✓		✓		✓
Accuracy					
Information has been verified.	✓	✓			
Corrections have been made based on tools.	✓		✓		✓
Information reflects the current product.	✓	✓	✓		✓
Information on a topic is consistent.	✓	✓	✓		✓
References to related information are correct.	✓		✓		✓
Completeness					
Only needed topics are covered.	✓	✓	✓		
Each topic has just the detail users need.	✓	✓	✓		
Patterns of information ensure proper coverage.	✓	✓	✓		✓
Information is repeated only when needed.	✓		✓		
Easy to Understand					
Clarity					
Focus is on meaning.	✓	✓	✓	✓	✓
Language is unambiguous.	✓		✓		✓
Elements are short.	✓		✓		✓

Table 6. Who Checks Which Quality Characteristics (Part 2 of 3)

Quality Characteristic and Guidelines	Writers	Technical Reviewers	Technical Editors	Graphic Designers	Peer Editors
Elements flow from one to another.	✓		✓		
Similar topics are presented in similar way.	✓		✓		
Technical terms are necessary and apt.	✓		✓		
New terms are defined.	✓		✓		✓
Concreteness					
Examples are appropriate for audience and topic.	✓	✓	✓		
Examples are realistic, accurate, up to date.	✓	✓	✓		✓
Examples are easy to find.	✓		✓	✓	✓
Scenarios illustrate tasks, provide overviews.	✓		✓		✓
Code examples are easy to adapt.	✓	✓	✓		✓
Unfamiliar information is related to familiar.	✓	✓	✓		
Style					
Grammar, spelling, punctuation are correct.	✓		✓		✓
Style guidelines are followed.	✓		✓	✓	✓
Style is active.	✓		✓		✓
Instructions are in the imperative mood.	✓		✓		✓
Tone is appropriate and consistent.	✓		✓		✓
Easy to Find					
Organization					
Organization of guidance information is sequential.	✓		✓		
Organization of reference information is logical.	✓		✓		

275

Table 6. Who Checks Which Quality Characteristics (Part 3 of 3)

Quality Characteristic and Guidelines	Writers	Technical Reviewers	Technical Editors	Graphic Designers	Peer Editors
Organization of information is consistent.	✓		✓		
Help is organized into discrete topics and types.	✓		✓		
Emphasis and subordination are appropriate.	✓		✓		
Topics are divided into at least two subtopics.	✓		✓		✓
Branches are used only if helpful.	✓		✓		
Users can see how pieces fit together.	✓		✓		
Retrievability					
Text is broken into manageable chunks.	✓		✓	✓	✓
Index has predictable entries.	✓	✓	✓		✓
Index is complete and correct.	✓		✓		✓
Linked-to information is easy to find.	✓		✓	✓	
Introductory sections reveal order.	✓		✓		
Table of contents has appropriate detail.	✓		✓	✓	✓
Key terms are easy to find.	✓		✓	✓	
Visual Effectiveness					
Visual elements are balanced.	✓		✓	✓	
Graphics are meaningful and appropriate.	✓	✓	✓	✓	
Illustrations complement text.	✓	✓	✓	✓	✓
Textual elements are a legible size and font.	✓		✓	✓	✓
Visual elements are used for emphasis.	✓		✓	✓	✓
Visual elements are logical and consistent.	✓		✓	✓	✓
Color and shading are discreet and significant.	✓		✓	✓	
Visual cues help users find what they need.	✓	✓	✓	✓	✓

Quality Characteristics and Elements

Many technical writing books are organized around information elements. They deal with what to do and not do at the level of words, sentences, tables, and so on.

Table 7, "Quality Characteristics and Elements," on page 279 shows how the quality characteristics apply to these elements.

Looking at the quality characteristics

Some quality characteristics operate mainly from the bottom up. Large semantic elements have the quality characteristic because the small elements do. You need to focus on the small elements to ensure that information has these quality characteristics:

❑ Accuracy
❑ Clarity
❑ Concreteness

Some quality characteristics operate more from the top down. You need to consider the large semantic elements to ensure that information has these quality characteristics:

❑ Completeness
❑ Organization
❑ Task orientation

Some quality characteristics are pervasive. They apply to every element. You can use various techniques at all levels of elements to enhance these quality characteristics:

❑ Retrievability
❑ Style
❑ Visual effectiveness

Looking at the elements

Few elements participate in all the characteristics. Examples are a notable exception, underlining their importance.

We can recognize semantic elements by their content, and we recognize syntactic elements by their form.

In Table 7, the following symbols are used:

✓ = A characteristic that is especially important for the given element.
x = A characteristic that is important for the given element.

Table 7. Quality Characteristics and Elements (Part 1 of 2)

Structure (from syntactic elements to semantic elements)	Quality Characteristics								
	Accuracy	Clarity	Completeness	Concreteness	Organization	Retrievability	Style	Task Orientation	Visual Effectiveness
Small elements—mainly syntactic									
Word, phrase	x	✓		x		x	x		
Sentence	x	✓		x		x	÷		
Paragraph	x	x	x		✓	x	x	x	x
Heading, title	x	x			x	✓	x	✓	x
List, ordered	x	✓	x	x		x	x	✓	x
List, unordered	x	✓	x	x		x	x		x
Table	x	x	x	x		✓	x	x	x
Figure, illustration, screen capture	x	x	x	✓		x	x		✓
Larger elements—mainly from book paradigm									
Title, edition notice, trademarks	x	✓					x		
Table of contents	x		x		x	✓	x	x	x
Introduction, summary, transition	x	x			✓	✓	x		x
Cross-reference, link, or citation	✓		x		✓	✓	x		
Glossary	x	x	✓			x	x		x
Bibliography	x		x			✓	x		x
Index	x	x	x			✓	x		x

Table 7. Quality Characteristics and Elements (Part 2 of 2)

Structure (from syntactic elements to semantic elements)	Quality Characteristics								
	Accuracy	Clarity	Completeness	Concreteness	Organization	Retrievability	Style	Task Orientation	Visual Effectiveness
Variable elements—mainly semantic									
Example	x	x	x	✓	x	x	x	x	x
Analogy, simile	x	x		✓			x		
Scenario	x	x	x	✓			x	✓	x
Term, definition, concept	x	✓	x	x		x	x		x
Instruction, guideline, hint, wizard, cue card	x	x	x	x	x	x	x	✓	x
Message	x	x	x	x		x	x	✓	
Description (as of process, classification)	x	✓	x	x		x			
Large semantic elements									
Guidance building block (module, article, topic, help window)			x		x	x	x	✓	x
Reference building block (module, article, topic, help window)	✓		x	x	x	✓	x		x
Guidance composite (such as guide, task help, tutorial)			x		x	x	x	✓	x
Reference composite (such as reference, contextual help)	✓		x	x	x	✓	x		x

Words to Watch for Clarity

Make every word count. Eliminate words that are not essential to the meaning. Replace words that are imprecise, ambiguous, negative, roundabout, or repetitive with words that precise, clear, positive, concise, and succinct.

This appendix lists many of these kinds of words to look out for and possible replacements for them.

Intensifying words

You might be able to eliminate some words entirely, such as:

absolutely	any	basically	certainly
definitively	just	of course	particularly
really	significantly	simply	some
specifically	very		

Such words are meant to intensify the meaning, but you'll probably find that the meaning is clearer without them. In speaking, people tend to use these words liberally, but they quickly lose their effect in writing. Try the sentence in your mind with and without the intensifying word, considering its effect in the larger context.

Imprecise verbs

Imprecision in a verb arises when the verb depends on a word or two after it to give it meaning. As you can see in the following list, the meaning of the verb moves to these other words or to the combination of words. Information is clearer when a verb conveys the action.

Imprecise Verbs	Precise Verbs
draws a conclusion	infers, concludes
gives rise to	causes
has a requirement; has plans	requires; plans
has the capability, is capable	can
is in agreement	agrees
makes contact with	meets
performs the printing	prints
provides assistance	helps
renders inoperative	breaks
makes changes to, makes use of	changes, uses

Words that can be hard to translate

Use words that have clear meanings. Be on the alert for other ways that some words might be understood, particularly by non-native speakers.

Ambiguous	Clear
as	because
as long as	provided that, if
in spite of	regardless of, despite
may	can, might
once	after, when
on the other hand	however, alternatively
since	because
through	finished
while	although, whereas

Negative expressions

There are several kinds of negative words. The more obvious ones are *no, not, none, never,* and *nothing.* Common combinations with *not* are:

Negative Expressions	Positive Expressions
not many	few
not the same	different
not different	similar
not unlike	like
not exclude	include
not. . . until	only when
not. . . unless	only if

Another common way for negatives to get into a sentence is through the negative prefix, which is attached to the beginning of a word:

de-, dis-	detach, deactivate, deemphasize, disentangle, disable, disagree
ex-	exclude, extinct, extinguish
in-, ir-	ineffective, inefficient, ineligible, inflexible irregular, irresponsible
non-	nonexistent, nonrestricted, nonsecure
re-	reduce, refuse, reject, reverse
un-	unavailable, undo, unlike, unpredictable, unrelated

Other negative words that are less obvious have negative meanings, though their form looks positive: *avoid, limit, wrong, fail, doubt.*

Some negatives cannot be turned into positives. However, replacing *not* combinations with one word (even though a negative word), usually makes sentences easier to understand.

Negative Expressions	Positive Expressions
does not	fails to
does not have	lacks
does not allow	prevents
does not accept	rejects
not able	unable
not possible	impossible

Roundabout expressions

Roundabout expressions tend to grow up around prepositions. Be suspicious when several words clump together, and consider whether one word might do.

Roundabout Expressions	Concise Terms
at this (that) point in time	now (then)
due to the fact that	because
during the course of	during
given the condition that	if
in the event that	if (*or* when)
in case of a	in a
in conjunction with	with
in order to	to
of an unusual nature	unusual
on account of the fact that	because
a variety of	various (*maybe* different, many, several *or nothing*)

Needless repetition

Some words are often used together, especially in speaking, but their meaning is so close that one word is enough. Cut away the excess.

Needless Repetition	Succinct Expressions
adequate enough	enough (*or* adequate)
create a new . . .	create a . . .
group together	group
involved, complex	complex
new innovation	innovation
one and only one	one
plan in advance, advance planning	plan, planning
share in common	share
sequential steps	steps
subject matter	subject
exactly the same	the same

Words derived from Latin

Latinate words contribute to a formal tone in writing. They usually have more syllables and seem less direct.

Words Derived from Latin	Words Derived from Anglo-Saxon
additional	more
discover	find
initiate	begin, start
majority	most
modify	change
perform	do
prior to	before

Bibliography

General

Brockmann, R. John. *Writing Better Computer User Documentation: From Paper to Hypertext*. Version 2. New York: John Wiley & Sons, Inc., 1990.

This book includes descriptions of reader-based writing techniques (such as using examples and metaphors and using a conversational style), structured writing, and editing, along with descriptions of related research. It has a comprehensive bibliography.

...For Dummies Computer Book Series. Foster City, CA: International Data Group.

This series of computer books presents information, in a sometimes comical style, for novice through intermediate users. This series is very popular, and you might look at how it presents technical information.

Horton, William. *Designing and Writing Online Documentation*. Second Edition. New York: John Wiley & Sons, Inc., 1994.

This book is a general style guide for designers and developers of online information. It is a very thorough guide that covers planning, user interface design, navigation and linking, and many other concepts and facets of online documentation.

Morrison, Deborah. *IBM's Official Guide to Building a Better Web Site*. Foster City, CA: IDG Books Worldwide, 1995.

Although this book includes information on administering a Web site and on HTML tags, much of the book deals with writing for the Web. The chapter on designing information for the Web includes rules of thumb for Web information such as "be brief" and "use complete headings."

Price, Jonathan, and Henry Korman. *How to Communicate Technical Information: A Handbook of Software and Hardware Documentation*. Redwood City, CA: The Benjamin/Cummings Publishing Company, Inc., 1993.

With lots of realistic advice and examples, this book deals with the process of developing technical information from planning and gathering information to reviewing it. This book includes chapters on developing particular kinds of technical information, such as tutorials and online help. It also briefly discusses how to implement the minimalist approach.

Easy to Use

Coe, Marlana. *Human Factors for Technical Communicators*. New York: John Wiley & Sons, Inc., 1996.

This book is a somewhat academic overview of the field of human factors as it applies to technical communication. It offers a good grounding in the prevailing theories of sensation and perception, learning, memory, problem solving, and information access mechanisms. It then makes recommendations for using this background information to choose a presentation medium and to design and develop usable information.

Dumas, J.S., and J.C. Redish. *A Practical Guide to Usability Testing*. Norwood, NJ: Ablex Publishing Corporation, 1994.

This book covers several methodologies for integrating usability testing into the development process. The focus is on overall product usability, including documentation.

Object-Oriented Interface Design: IBM Common User Access Guidelines. First Edition. Carmel, IN: Que Corporation, 1992.

This book documents the design principles and terminology for user interfaces that conform to Common User Access (CUA).

Weiss, Edmond H. *How to Write Usable User Documentation*. Second Edition. Phoenix, AZ: Oryx Press, 1991.

> In addition to showing how to design, develop, test, and maintain modules, this book deals with some clarity and retrievability issues.

Easy to Understand

The Associated Press Stylebook. Reading, MA: Addison-Wesley, 1984.

> The *AP Stylebook* is the primary style reference at many newspapers and magazines. In a single alphabetical list, it covers capitalization, punctuation, word usage, and other style topics. It gives good advice in many areas, but remember that the news media use slightly different conventions than technical publications do.

Blake, Gary, and Robert W. Bly. *The Elements of Technical Writing*. New York: Macmillan, 1993.

> Modeled roughly on *The Elements of Style*, this book characterizes good technical writing as technically accurate; useful; concise; complete; clear; consistent; correct in spelling, punctuation, and grammar; targeted; well organized; and interesting. The book includes 50 rules, 39 of them on the use of numbers, units of measure, equations, symbols, punctuation, grammar, abbreviations, and capitalization.

Brogan, John A. *Clear Technical Writing*. New York: McGraw-Hill, 1973.

> This book is packed with examples and exercises for learning how to eliminate "gobbledygook" from your writing. It focuses on major sources of unclear writing, such as redundancies, weak verbs, abstract nouns, showy writing, and improper subordination.

The Chicago Manual of Style. 14th ed. Chicago and London: University of Chicago Press, 1993.

> This style guide is the most widely used general reference on matters of academic and technical style. It has chapters devoted to topics such as punctuation, numbers, and indexes. However, it focuses on printed information, not online information.

Microsoft Manual of Style for Technical Publications. Redmond, WA: Microsoft Press, 1995.

> This style guide for writers documenting Microsoft products and technologies is arranged alphabetically. It has entries from "abbreviations and acronyms" to "zoom in, zoom out." This manual often provides a rationale for its guidelines, emphasizing clarity and consistency, and can apply more broadly to the computer industry.

United Press International Stylebook. Chicago: National Textbook Company, 1992.

Although intended for the print and broadcast media, the *UPI Stylebook* is an easy-to-use, alphabetical quick reference for spelling, word selection, and punctuation. It gives good advice in many areas, but remember that the news media use slightly different conventions than technical publications do.

Williams, Joseph M. *Style: Ten Lessons in Clarity and Grace*. Second Edition. Glenview, IL: Scott, Foresman and Company, 1985.

Although this book has a broader focus than just technical information, its lessons on coherence, emphasis, and conciseness are valuable for technical writers. The book has many examples and an in-depth analysis of them.

Easy to Find

Bonura, Larry S. *The Art of Indexing*. New York: John Wiley & Sons, 1994.

The bible on indexing, this book has even a sample style guide for indexing. Bonura offers five criteria for a good index: accuracy, depth of indexing, conciseness, cross-references, and logical headings. Bonura also emphasizes knowing your audience.

Horton, William. *Illustrating Computer Documentation: The Art of Presenting Information Graphically on Paper and Online*. New York: John Wiley & Sons, 1991.

This book is a comprehensive work on why and how to integrate graphics with computer documentation, covering both printed and online information. It is articulate and complete, replete with illustrations and examples, and follows its own guidelines well.

Horton, William. *The Icon Book*. New York: John Wiley & Sons, 1996.

This book is an excellent guide for designers of icons for graphical user interfaces. It includes extensive recommendations for things to consider when designing for specific audiences, including international and cultural considerations.

Lopuck, Lisa. *Designing Multimedia: A Visual Guide to Multimedia and Online Graphic Design*. Berkeley, CA: Peachpit Press, 1996.

> Although the main focus of this book is on multimedia, it offers a good set of guidelines for visual designers on the planning, designing, and development of online graphic media, including user interface design and design for the Web. It includes information on the technical hurdles of designing for multiple operating systems, hardware, software, and color palettes. It deals with handling production issues, and even how to get design jobs and set fees.

Pfeiffer, William S. *Technical Writing: A Practical Approach*. Third Edition. Prentice Hall, 1997.

> This book devotes an unusual amount of attention to organization. It has a couple chapters on methods of organizing information, including induction and deduction.

Weinman, Lynda. *Designing Web Graphics: How to Prepare Images and Media for the Web*. Indianapolis, IN: New Riders Publishing, 1996.

> This book provides a wealth of vital information for creators of graphics for the Web. It provides technical guidance on how to work within the constraints of varying Web browsers, color palettes, and operating systems. Some guidance on good design of graphics, type, and page layout is included. Also included is a CD containing many sample files as well as several shareware programs to assist with Web graphic design.

Wilson, Stephen. *World Wide Web Design Guide*. Hayden Books, 1995.

> This book by an artist and designer concentrates on visual aspects of information on the Web. The chapter on the challenge of Web design offers a model for analyzing good Web design and includes tips on organizing information as well as making information visually appealing.

Glossary

A

abbreviation. A shortened form of a word or phrase, used in place of the whole. Unlike acronyms, abbreviations should be pronounceable as words, can end in a period, and might not be all uppercase. For example, Calif. is an abbreviation for California.

accuracy. Freedom from mistake or error; adherence to fact or truth.

acronym. A word formed from the first letter of each part or of each major part of a compound term. For example, CAD stands for computer-aided design.

analogy. An explicit comparison based on a resemblance between things that are otherwise not alike.

artificial task. A task that is imposed by a product or presented in terms of using a product component. For example, "using the CNTREC utility" is artificial; but "counting records with the CNTREC utility" is not. Contrast with *real task*.

audience. A group of readers who have similar tasks and a similar background; they may have differing expertise in performing these tasks.

B

beta test. A test of a pre-release version of a product, usually involving customers outside the company. An earlier test, usually involving users within the company, is an alpha test.

branch. A jump to another place in the information, usually marked by a link or cross-reference. A user can choose to go to the other information or not to go. See also *link*.

C

chunk. (noun) A logical unit of information that addresses only one topic and allows modularity of the information. (verb) To group information into discrete parts based on content, and label each part, or chunk.

clarity. Freedom from ambiguity or obscurity.

completeness. The inclusion of all necessary parts—and only those parts.

conceptual information. Information that pertains to design, ideas, relationships, and definitions.

concreteness. The inclusion of appropriate examples, scenarios, similes, and analogies.

contextual help. Online information that is relevant to where the user is in a program. Contextual help typically includes information about a particular window or field.

cue card. A type of online information that provides an overview of possible tasks and guides users to instructions for the task that they choose.

E

element. A unit that physically constitutes technical information. Such a unit can be, for example, a word, heading, paragraph, list, or tutorial.

entry point. An element that marks the presence and location of information. An entry point can be, for example, a heading, index, hypertext link, or table of contents.

example. A representative of a set of things. In technical writing, an example can be code, text (such as a scenario), or a graphic.

expert user. A person whose experience and maybe also training makes the person comfortable using a tool and able to handle most tasks. Compare with *novice user* and *user*.

F

field test. A test of a product in an actual or simulated work environment before releasing the product.

figure. An illustration, chart, or diagram inserted into a block of textual information to complement or clarify that information. Figures are usually, but not always, labeled.

font. In printing and publishing, a complete set of letters, numbers, and punctuation of a particular design and size; one size of a *typeface*.

G

gerund. A verbal that ends in *-ing* and functions as a noun. A gerund can have objects, complements, or modifiers.

graphic. An illustration or small icon that depicts or is associated with a fact or concept or a particular type of information.

graphical element. Any non-textual visual element that is intentionally added to text to enhance its visual impact.

graphical user interface (GUI). A type of user interface that takes advantage of high-resolution graphics. A graphical user interface typically combines graphics, object-action paradigm, pointing device, menu bars, menus, overlapping windows, and icons.

guidance information. Information that explains how to do a task. It includes procedures, examples, concepts, and relationships.

H

heading. A prominent phrase or word that describes the information following it. In this book, marginal phrases that help retrievability are also considered headings.

help. Discrete pieces of online information about parts of a product such as a window, field, message, or task.

hypertext. An organization of online information that is like a network rather than a hierarchy. Users can browse information using links. See also *link*.

I

illustration. A drawing, painting, diagram, or photograph used to explain, depict, or complement text.

indention. The blank space between a margin and the beginning of an indented line.

interface. The means by which users interact with computer hardware and software.

internationalization. The process of taking something developed within the context of a certain culture and translating it for another culture. This includes ensuring that graphics and examples are appropriate, as well as translating the words.

J

jargon. Technical terminology or characteristic idiom of a science, trade, profession, or similar group.

L

link. A technique used in online information for giving users an opportunity to jump to related information without having to search for it. Links provide the connections among pieces of information in hypertext. See also *hypertext*.

M

message. Information that a user does not request but that a product or application displays. Information messages give status. Error messages give a warning or information about an unexpected event.

metaphor. A word, phrase, or visual representation that denotes or depicts one object or idea but suggests a likeness to or analogy with another object or idea.

multimedia. A computer application that uses any combination of text, image, animation, video and audio effects to present information to the user.

N

navigate. In online information, to use controls available in the interface to display a different portion of the information.

novice user. Someone who has little or no experience in a particular area. Compare with *expert user* and *user*.

O

organization. A coherent arrangement of parts that makes sense to the user.

P

parallelism. Using the same grammatical structure for similar elements such as items in a list, nouns or adjectives in a series, and compound clauses.

pattern. A form or model for dealing with recurring kinds of elements. A pattern might include headings for various kinds of information and the layout for information under those headings.

pixel. An abbreviation of "picture element": the smallest single point on a display screen that can be assigned an individual color value.

point. A standard unit of type size; the British and American standard is 72 points to an inch.

pseudo-task heading. A heading that masks a real task or that makes a conceptual or reference section seem to be a task section.

Q

quality. Excellence or superiority in kind.

quality characteristic. An attribute essential to describing quality.

R

real task. A task users want to perform, whether they use your product to do it or not. For example, "balancing your checkbook" is a real task; "using InfoBanker's Balance feature" is not. Contrast with *artificial task*.

reference information. A collection of facts (such as terms, statements, commands, rules, messages, names of windows and buttons, conventions) that are organized for quick retrieval.

resolution. The dimensions in pixels of the display area of a computer monitor. *Low* resolution is 640 pixels wide by 480 pixels high. *High* resolution is 1024 pixels by 768 pixels or higher. Text on a monitor set to 640x480 resolution will appear larger than the same text on the same monitor set to 1024x768, because the pixels that make up the text occupy a smaller relative portion of the screen in the higher resolution format.

retrievability. Presentation of information in a way that enables users to find specific items quickly and easily.

S

sans serif. Of or relating to a typeface whose letters do not include small terminal strokes (serifs) at the end of the main strokes of the letters.

scenario. A series of events over time, usually around a fictitious but realistic set of circumstances.

semantic. Of or relating to meaning; used here especially as expressed through the elements of technical information. Compare with *syntactic*.

serif. (1) The small terminal stroke at the end of the main stroke of a letter. (2) Of or relating to a typeface whose letters all include such small terminal strokes.

sidebar. Additional material, displayed in marked-off boxes, that usually provides a different level of detail than the primary information.

simile. An explicit comparison (often introduced by *like* or *as*) of two things to show a similarity they share.

slab serif. (1) A heavy or squared serif that is almost the same thickness as the main stroke to which it is attached. (2) Of or relating to a typeface with thick, squared serifs.

style. Correctness and appropriateness of writing conventions and choices of words and phases.

syntactic. Of or relating to syntax as the harmonious arrangement of elements. Compare with *semantic*.

T

task. An activity, physical or mental, that is done with a product (such as editing a file) or for a product (such as installing and maintaining the product).

task analysis. The process of determining primarily who does a task and how, but also when, where, and why.

task help. Online information that provides guidance on how to perform a task with a product.

task orientation. A focus on helping users complete tasks associated with a product in relation to their jobs.

technical information. The information that accompanies a product (for sale or not) or system or describes something in a science (whether computer science, physical science, or social science), trade, or profession.

technical writing. The process of writing, reviewing, and revising technical information.

term. A word or expression that is peculiar to a science, art, profession, or subject.

typeface. A complete set of letters, numbers, and punctuation of a particular design: for example, Helvetica or Times Roman.

type size. The nominal size of a font, in points. This size usually includes a small amount of blank space, or *shoulder*, above and below the actual printed character. Thus, the printed words in a line of 12-point type might be only 10.5 points high.

U

usability. The ease with which people in a defined group can learn and use a product (including the information) to accomplish certain tasks.

usability test. A test of the interaction between the user and the product or information for the product.

user. A person who comes in contact with a product through doing any of the following tasks with or for the product: evaluating, planning, buying, learning, installing, using, operating, administering, developing applications, customizing, diagnosing, or maintaining. See also *expert user* and *novice user*.

user interface. The area at which a user and an object come together to interact; as applied to computers, the ensemble of hardware and software that allows a user to interact with a computer. See also *graphical user interface*.

V

visual effectiveness. Attractiveness and enhanced meaning of information through use of layout, illustrations, color, type, icons, and other graphical devices.

visual element. Any component of a block of information that affects the visual impact of the information. A visual element could be, for example, highlighting, a heading, table, or illustration.

W

Web site. A collection of directories and files on a server that can be accessed by users with Web browsers.

white space. The portion of a printed page or online window that is left blank.

wizard. A type of interface (usually dialog boxes) that leads users through well-defined steps to produce a result, such as creating a chart from information in a database.

Index

E

Developing Quality Technical Information

Developing Quality Technical Information

S

T

U